eXXXit

John Hammer

Generation Culture Transformation
Specializing in publishing for generation culture change

eGenCo
824 Tallow Hill Road
Chambersburg, PA 17202, USA
Phone: 717-461-3436
Email: info@egen.co
Website: www.egen.co

facebook.com/egenbooks

youtube.com/egenpub

 egen.co/blog

Publisher's Cataloging-in-Publication Data
Publisher's Cataloging-in-Publication Data
Hammer, John
eXXXit; by John Hammer.
180 pages cm.
ISBN: 978-1-936554-84-3 paperback
   978-1-936554-85-0 ebook
   978-1-936554-86-7 ebook
1. Pornography. 2. Sexual addiction. 3. Christian Counseling. J. I. Title
2014943281

Cover design and interior layout by Kevin Lepp, KML Studio.

Author's Note

All stories contained herein are true and factual to the best of my knowledge. Most of the names have been changed to protect the privacy of the individuals involved.

The issue of pornography and sexual sin is an epidemic that faces men and women both young and old. Statistics tell us that men more commonly struggle with pornography than do women. However, pornography use by women is becoming more and more common. In *eXXXit*, my heart's intention is to address this issue for both men and women of all ages. Although the discussion overall may seem to be directed a little more towards men than women, I believe that both genders will benefit from this information. Please forgive me if this causes any offense.

Table of Contents

Endorsements

God wants to heal and forgive sexual sins and brokenness. Motivated by love, John Hammer has written a book that will be the best weapon you have to kill the giant of pornography. It's biblical! It's practical! It's motivational! Become a freedom fighter by first becoming free.

Leif Hetland
President, Global Mission Awareness
Author of *Seeing Through Heaven's Eyes*
http://globalmissionawareness.com

There is no fullness without cleansing. We cannot reach the heights of what the Father wants for us if Christ has not plumbed the depths of who he is for us.

John's book is an honest, open account of one person's story of coming fully into the light of God's power and blessing. It can be your journey also as you work through the exercises and allow the Holy Spirit to touch your heart, reframe your thinking, and replace your addiction with a fresh passion for Jesus.

Even now, God is surrounding you with *his* zeal for your righteousness. You're going to make it!

Graham Cooke
Author and Speaker
www.brilliantperspectives.com
www.brilliantbookhouse.com

I highly recommend John Hammer's very well written book, which tells his story of struggle against the highly addictive problem of pornography and his path to total freedom. The practical prayers and pointers throughout the book are invaluable. One of the heroes of the book is his dad, whose counsel steered him on the right path every time. As a deliverance minister, pornography has been a common issue I have encountered, and John handles the subject of strongholds attached to this addiction very well. This book is so needed today throughout the Body of Christ—my hope is that it is widely circulated for decades to come.

Doris M. Wagner
Minister, Global Spheres Inc.

---

eXXXit is a war manual that will equip this generation to confront and conquer the raging battle against sexual sin. In his book, author John Hammer paints a clear picture of God's intention for our sexuality, the war against God's intended purpose, and the power of the gospel to restore all who seek real and lasting freedom. If you struggle to understand your sexuality, this book is for you! If you struggle with pornography, this is book is for you! If you need a resource to help people obtain freedom from pornography or any form of sexual impurity, this book is for you! I am convinced that everyone who reads this book will be strengthened by sound biblical teaching and compelled by incredible testimonies of God›s healing and delivering power. Through the Gospel of Jesus Christ, there is hope and freedom, so get ready to make an *eXXXit*!

Ben Dixon
Director of 11th Hour Ministries
Author of *Hearing God*
www.11thhourministries.org

eXXXit is a tool for the hand of the revivalist who seeks to make the crooked paths straight and the rough places plain, that the glory of the Lord may be revealed. I'm thrilled to see a uniquely gospel-centered work target the high places of our culture. May the power of the gospel be released and a thousand more voices like that of John Hammer emerge in this generation to give great light in an hour of darkness.

Adam Narciso
Pioneer and Director, Catalyst Training School
www.adamnarciso.com

John Hammer writes about sexual purity in such a profound way; every pastor, leader, and teacher needs to get their hands on this book. *eXXXit* addresses both the spiritual and practical implications of what it means to walk in victory over pornography. Writing with integrity about a subject that largely goes unaddressed in the pulpits of our churches takes immense courage and transparency. John writes this book from the perspective of someone who struggled, found Jesus, found freedom, and now has a desire to help others find their way. I highly recommend *eXXXit* by John Hammer for those who want information and tools on how to get free, stay free, and speak with knowledge and conviction on the area of sexual purity. Read this book today—it will be one of the best decisions you ever make.

Pastor Russell Johnson
Youth and Young Adult Pastor
Cedar Park Church/TheExchange
@russellbjohnson

John has addressed the topic of the dangers of pornography in a day when this epidemic is out of control. Countless lives are being tragically impacted by this hideous addiction. John has not only addressed the issue, but he brings tremendous help to the reader. He offers tools that will set people free and articulates the power of God and his deliverance.

Wayde Goodall, DMin
Dean, College of Ministry
Associate Professor of Church Leadership
Director, Graduate Programs
Northwest University
northwestu.edu

There are a few "unspoken" topics among Christians that aren't preached from the pulpit or even discussed in small groups. One of those is pornography. With raw transparency, John Hammer chronicles his own struggle as a young man as he made his way through the labyrinth of hiddenness, guilt, shame, and finally to deliverance through Christ. Prepare to be challenged by the sheer statistics related to this issue and allow your heart to be softened towards those caught in its grip. John's book not only paints an accurate and well-researched picture of pornography in our culture; it also offers hope, a way out, an *eXXXit* from an addiction destroying countless lives and families. Read this book, then buy several copies to give away. And if you've been caught in the snare of pornography, by all means, read this book! It will change your life.

Jane Hansen Hoyt
President and CEO
Aglow International
www.aglow.org

Everyone has problems. Yet so few want to admit their problems or even help others overcome their shortcomings for fear that it would make them look imperfect as well. Many youth and youth leaders would rather be seen as perfect from afar than to be open and walk in wholeness.

This book is an invitation to wholeness via openness. It's a discussion based in honesty and the possibilities brought about by vulnerability.

I applaud my friend John for taking the time to write with passion, humility, and grace on a topic that has taken so many down.

I highly recommend this book to individuals, leaders, and small groups.

Wes Dunn
Speaker
@wesdunn

Christ is returning for a pure and radiant Bride: holy and blameless (Eph. 5:25-27). This means the prevalent porn addiction the church is currently experiencing will virtually be non-existent. I firmly believe this book will equip the people of God to walk in the freedom Christ died on the cross for. John presents the path from "pain to porn to purity" in an honest, straightforward, and biblical way. Using insights from both Scripture and experience, John shows us that the *eXXXit* from porn is actually possible.

Richie Cruz
Founder of Porn Scar
http://pornscar.com

eXXXit is a candid, compassionate, solution-oriented resource to be read by any person ready to begin a life of liberty and joy found in communion with the true and living God of the universe. John Hammer paints a clear picture of the dangers and destructive nature of addiction.

Andre Benjamin
Founder: CEO OF DESTINY, LLC
Author of *It's Your Future*
www.itsyourfuturetour.com

As I was reading through *eXXXit*, I came across phrases like, "My goal is not to focus on how much pornography we can escape from but how much of Jesus we can put on," and "Taking the *eXXXit* isn't about seeing how great we are but allowing people to see how great Jesus is." I found this to be very encouraging! This is not a book on how we have to work to overcome, but how Jesus already overcame for us. The battle is already won. In *eXXXit*, the focus is squarely on Jesus, where it should be.

I really appreciate how transparent and real John is in this book. He really helps the reader feel safe and relaxed and to realize that he is not alone. *eXXXit* explains clearly not only how pornography sucks you in and the negative effects it has on you, but also how to get freedom from pornography forever and live practically in victory on a daily basis.

I strongly recommend this book to anyone struggling with pornography or anyone who wants to help someone who is struggling.

Meesh Fomenko
The City Church, Ventura, CA
Meesh Fomenko International

Dedication

I am dedicating this book to the men who God brought into my life to encourage me and help me when I first began to experience the freedom that is in Jesus Christ. There are many other men and women that helped me along the way, but in my first few years of freedom these men stepped into my life and weren't afraid to walk with me and believe in me. I am so thankful for all you have done for me. I love you guys!

Dad, you convinced me that I was lovable and your patient example and encouragement got me through many dark days. I wouldn't be the man that I am today without you. Thanks for following Jesus and paying the price so that I could have such a rich inheritance in Christ.

Todd Bevan, you were really there for me and helped me not to be such a headcase. You helped pull the best out of me and spoke into my destiny. You mean so much to me.

Russ Babcock, thank you for being a great youth pastor and friend to me. Thanks for helping me have a place to serve as I got back on my feet, and for letting me share this message so often with our young people at Sonrise.

Bob McGowan, you added serious strength to me at many key times when I felt defeated. Thanks for your prophetic passion and support.

Richard Marciel, you had the most mysterious and subtle way of dropping life-changing truth on me. I know the Father's tenderness and love in a greater way because of your influence. I want to love God more when I am around you.

Darin Leonard, God used you to restore my heart as a man, utilizing simple things like deep conversations, teaching me how to use tools, and trusting me to problem-solve. I am so blessed that God brought me into your business for a season. I wouldn't be who I am today without my time serving you.

Mike Stansberry, you were a huge encouragement to me as I started Bible college. You listened to and encouraged me a lot. You helped me feel sane. Your prayers and prophetic encouragement went a long way.

John Fuller, you gave me keys that still help guide my life today. I am really blessed that you invested in me and helped me build confidence.

Dr. Matthew Thomas, I am so thankful for your transparency and encouragement over the years. Your wisdom has helped me practically as a leader in many areas. You convinced me that God was not through with me when I felt I was at my lowest point.

Ben Dixon, I am thankful that God brought you into my life. I appreciate being able to be real with you and to have you sharpen me in so many ways. You came alongside to help me really get breakthrough and embrace my identity in Christ.

Acknowledgments

I am so thankful for everyone who has helped shape my life and helped me shape this book. Thank you Vish and Marti, as well as the whole team at eGen. You have been a blessing to work with and I am so grateful for the quality product that you turned my book into. Thank you, Kevin, for the cover art, which communicates the book's message so effectively. Thank you, Steve, for cleaning up my manuscript and editing my work while preserving my voice throughout the text.

Thank you, Indiegogo Inc., for developing a platform that allows artists and innovators to raise funds and release their dreams.

Thank you Dad, Herb Marks, Doug Martin, Andre Benjamin, Ben Dixon, and Dr. Wayde Goodall for reading my manuscript and giving me feedback. Thank you, Herb, for your prophetic encouragement and insight through the process of getting this book launched. Thank you, Philip Martin, for the phone call and helping me clarify the link between pornography and human trafficking.

Thank you, Landon Schott, for connecting me with Marti, while we first met in India, and for opening the door for me to be published. Thank you, Andre Benjamin, for encouraging me to take risks with my creativity all along the way. Thank you for that car conversation after the Propaganda Show that helped me with the right title for this book. Thank you, Ben Dixon, for being a listening ear, a prophetic voice, and a trusted friend through this process. You are a true friend and I feel like I can never repay how much you bless me. Thank you, Russell Johnson, for being a good friend and for keeping me fired up all the time.

Thank you, Mom and Dad—Anna and David—for being such a great and supportive family. I am blessed to be placed in such an amazing family and am so thankful to God for you.

Thank you, Sonrise Christian Center, for embracing me, my passion, and my honesty. I have forged much of this message while I ministered with and to our church family. You see my best and worst and have created an atmosphere of encouragement for me to grow in. Thank you to the staff at Sonrise, for being so amazing to work with and an example of faithfulness to Jesus.

Thank you to our amazing friends who intercede for us! Your prayers over my family and ministry are so appreciated. I am deeply grateful for the love and time that you sacrifice to cover us in prayer. I am very thankful for your prayers, which are bearing much fruit through this whole process.

Thank you to Graham Cooke, Ben Dixon, Adam Narciso, Leif Hetland, Doris Wagner, Russell Johnson, Dr. Wayde Goodall, Jane Hansen, Richie Cruz, Wes Dunn, Meesh Fomenko and Andre Benjamin for writing endorsements for my book. I am so honored by your kind words. May God continue to bless the work that he has for each of you. Thank you, Dad, for the Foreword. It means a lot to be loved so much by my dad.

Thank you to my beautiful wife, Grace Elaine. You are my best friend and you have brought more joy into my life than I could have imagined. Thank you for listening, praying, laughing, and counseling me through this season of writing. Your sacrifice of allowing me the time to write is so generous. You are amazing and THE BEST!

Thank you for the greatest kids! I love you Hailey, Emma, Justus, and Addison! You guys move my heart like no one else. I believe in you and know that you guys will do greater things than your dad. I hope that you learn from my mistakes and successes and that you take risks in your life to make Jesus known in your generation.

Lastly, I truly want to thank God for being faithful to me. In my pain and shame, you were there. I have found you to be the most loving and good Father. You opened my eyes and filled my heart with love. I believed the Good News long ago, but I keep discovering that it is better than I could have ever imagined. Thank you for your grace, for without it I am nothing and have nothing of value to share with others. You have won my heart and I am forever grateful.

Indiegogo, Inc. Supporters

I will forever be grateful for each one of you that believed in me and in this project—to write a book on freedom from pornography. You partnered with me in a sacrificial and generous way that allowed this dream to become a reality. May God bless the dreams that he has put in your hearts. THANK YOU!

Jordan Watson
Len and Debbie Wiens
Carl Aardsma
Brian Stockdale
Eric and Shuree Hoffman
John and Carol Nemchick
Matt and Manesseh Ferrell
Russ and Kim Babcock
Keith and Pauline Batchelor
Ryan Pemberton
Caleb and Ariana Babcock
Bryan and Natalie Gaceta
John Sage
Landon Schott
Andy Toles
Andre and Ambra Benjamin
Lindsey Tuiasosopo
Dave and Carolyn Peterson

Jonathan Young
Donna Hart
Karen Williamson
Marrielle Tol
Jill and Randy Knight
Nathan and Cassie Johnson
Todd and Wendy Bevan
Jonathon Estrada
Kay Rogers
Andy Lubresky
Julie Ferguson
Emily Winslow
Ted and Sherrie Graves
David and Darcie Hammer
Rebecca Sargent
Andrew Branson
Scott Dotson
Brenda Super
Diane and Chuck Fink
Eric Johnson
Michael Lee
Scott and Brie Chaussee
Patricia Graef
Phil Manginelli
Jason Fay
Annie Austin
Dad and Mom
Perry Hargrave
Ben and Brigit Dixon
Eric and Carrie Olsen
Pat and Deanna Brenner
John and Brianna Burt
Janine Reiser
Chris Manginelli

Indiegogo, Inc. Supporters

Janice Le
Ryan Hoxsey
Mateja Avarmovic
Byllie Ricketts
Shane Wynn
Tina Sander
Micheal and Jaclyn Miller
Dennis and Jamie Sovern
Sue and Daryl Thomson
Martyn and Anita Young
Rob and Debby Werdell
Ben Millard
Tom and Debbie Gibbons
Byron Eggehorn
Gloria Van Gent
Micah Patdu
Michelle Patdu
James Young
Anonymous*

*Hopefully I did not overlook anyone, but if I did I apologize and I am grateful for you too!

Foreword

Every second, over three thousand dollars is spent on pornography.

eXXXit is a real look at the effects of pornography on one man's life and exposes the statistics of a multi-million dollar industry's far-and-wide-reaching impact on the world.

This generation is vulnerable and at high risk due to the ease and availability of pornography via the Internet. The author paints a picture of the tremendous need in our society for someone to stand up and lead the way out of this trap that the enemy would love to use as a weapon of destruction. "The thief comes only to steal, kill and destroy," but Jesus comes to give us life and life more abundantly (John 10:10).

John Hammer takes the very sensitive and long-ignored subject of pornography and displays the redemption of the Father in his own life while laying the foundation for freedom from this bondage and stronghold. The author reveals true and hard facts about the industry as well as his own struggle, showing the reader a life of victory over sin and temptation. One of those truths is the renewing and rewiring of the mind discussed in Chapter 9, without which there cannot be change.

I am very proud of my son and how he has allowed God to free him and work through him to bring change to people lives. *eXXXit* will show you the strategy you need to escape the enemy's plan and get on with God's destiny.

I love you John.

Dr. Dan C. Hammer
Sonrise Christian Center
Everett, Washington
Senior Pastor
John Hammer's Dad
isonrise.org

Introduction

eXXXit is a clarion call to live the abundant life, a life full of all that Christ has purchased for you on the cross. Pornography is a multi-billion dollar a year industry that not only robs the pocket books of earth's citizens but also enslaves them. As such, pornography is always a master and never a servant. The sex industry is a major dominating influence of the cultural norms in the 21st century.

Pornography instills in our youth unhealthy and twisted perceptions of sexual relationships, training men to be predators instead of protectors. It destroys marriages and enslaves women. Porn is so pervasive today that it is virtually impossible to completely avoid its influence. It's time for a revolution. It's time for freedom to come to the masses. It's time to free our families and free our children. It's time to turn the tide on what's considered normal when it comes to sexual experience. It's time to take the *eXXXit* and live a life of freedom.

eXXXit is really about the freedom that comes through Jesus Christ. My goal is not to focus on how much pornography we can escape from but how much of Jesus we can put on. As Paul wrote to the Romans, "The night is far spent, the day is at hand. Therefore let us cast off the works of darkness, and let us put on the armor of light. Let us walk properly, as in the day, not in revelry and drunkenness, not in lewdness and lust, not in strife and envy. But put on the Lord Jesus Christ, and make no provision for the flesh, to fulfill its lusts" (Rom. 13:12-14).

Freedom is not just a great idea; it's a promise from God Himself. In this book we will look into the Bible and discover that within its pages lies the power to break free any soul enslaved by the shackles of sexual immorality and pornography. The Bible's main purpose is to reveal the God-Man, Jesus Christ. Jesus came to save people from their sins. He came to liberate the human heart.

To dive into this book is to dive into the person and work of Christ. He holds the power to set your soul free. This is not an invitation to self-help. Self gets one into slavery. The gospel of Jesus brings one into freedom. The gospel not only brings you life after death, it also heals you and makes you whole.

My personal experience with pornography started around middle school. In 6th grade I started to have a little more curiosity about sexual things and I saw an advertisement for pornography. I wasn't really sure about much of anything at that point. I remember we even had a talk in our 6th grade class about sex and I remember feeling embarrassed and not able to comprehend what my teacher was talking about. Then by 7th grade, some of the other boys at my Christian school brought pornography to school and passed it around. From that point on pornography and sexual things were big topics of conversation for me and my peers throughout the rest of my teen years.

My parents did talk to me a little bit about sex and pornography. My pastors mentioned it a little bit at church. But looking back, I honestly do not believe that most church people in the 90s understood what an epidemic this problem really was becoming. For me at that time, however, as all this new information about sex was entering my life in my early teenage years, I was deceived with regard to the truth and decided to hide my newfound curiosity about women and sexual desire.

Because of my deception, my life over the next 7-8 years was riddled with lust and sexual immorality. What started as a little curiosity in middle school became a full-blown addiction. I woke up daily looking for ways to find pornography and live in a fantasy world. I went to church and Christian school but was a complete hypocrite. I looked down on people who partied and had sex outside of marriage. There was so much pride, deception and judgment in my life that I condemned other people in their sin even as I was the worst of sinners. I was living a double life, constantly exposed to the freedom that was available in Jesus but continually persisting in my bondage to sin.

Right before my 21st birthday, I finally hit rock bottom. I went to visit a friend one night and he wasn't home. Feeling alone and rejected, I drove to a couple of places nearby that sold pornography and looked around for a while just to feed my sinful desires. I didn't even buy anything. In the end I just went back home and headed straight to my room. Suddenly a sense of guilt and shame came upon me so heavily that I literally began to shake. Fear of what I had done overwhelmed me. I was about to take the *eXXXit*.

My bedroom was in the basement and my dad was watching a TV show just down the hall. I asked my dad to come to my room so we could talk. When we were alone together I started confessing part of what I had done that night and a little about the sin that I had given myself over to in the previous years. I was so afraid of being judged and rejected that I didn't think I could be fully honest. In the weeks and months that followed I found out that my fears of rejection were not based in reality. My dad and several other men with whom I began to confess my sin and talk about my emotional problems didn't reject me at all. They were proud of me for being honest and taking responsibility for my sin. At the same time, they never were easy on sin or let me think it was acceptable. Sometimes they corrected me, but mostly they encouraged me, challenged me and—most important of all—loved me. God used the power of confession in my life to start the process of healing and walking in freedom.

After the first month of confessing my sin and trusting Jesus to free me there was a huge change in my life. I woke up every morning with a passionate desire to resist the devil and honor God. My deepest desires had changed almost overnight... I still faced temptation and memories, but instead of just giving into immoral thoughts, I trusted Jesus to empower me to overcome them. My behavior changed as radically as my desires did. I didn't intentionally look for pornography at all anymore on the Internet or anywhere else. I started being careful of the music I listened to and the movies and television programs I watched. I started spending time in worship and prayer. My ever-increasing hunger for God drove me into my Bible as never before. I was desperate to know God's ways of purity. I can't count the times or days that I used to look at pornography or intentionally dream up sinful fantasies. Masturbation was a horrible addiction. And all of this was over. It became very evident that the grace of God had pursued me and changed the affections of my heart.

I don't mean to paint a picture that I was perfect at this time or that I am now. It's just a dramatic change in my life occurred when I identified that Jesus could set me free and I cried out to Him. Before Jesus liberated me, I thought I would be dominated by these sinful habits and behaviors for the rest of my life. One of my biggest struggles was dealing with the deep, heavy sense of shame I felt over my past. The devil was working overtime to drag me back into my old ways or to make me give up on thinking I could be forgiven.

I went through a battle with depression and guilt that lasted a couple of years, unable to see God as a loving Father who wanted to remove my shame. I felt like I had sinned so much as a Christian that there was no way God could really forgive me, since I had sinned willfully. My dad, my friends and the many mentors that helped me through this season were such a blessing. I couldn't be where I am today without them. Their counsel and their prayers for the devil's influence to be broken off my life were powerful and fruitful. But ultimately my freedom was not established and I could not live in peace until I embraced through faith the marvelous reality of God's grace. The message was that I was a sinner, but because of God's grace in sending Jesus to die for me, I could be accepted by God and forgiven of ALL my sins.

God continues to mold me and form me to be more like Jesus. My mind is renewed the more I spend time in God's presence and in His Word. Obeying God has not been an easy life but I have never regretted it. Many men have come to me for prayer and support. It gives me great joy to see men take the *eXXXit* out of porn and trust other men enough to open up about their sin. It's a major first step toward freedom.

I have written this book to testify to you that in Jesus as revealed in the Scriptures, you can be free from sexual immorality and live a life that glorifies God. I used to be tormented every day with thoughts of my past and certain temptations. I used to believe the lie that freedom was like a carrot that God was dangling from a stick to get me to move in the right direction but something I could not quite experience. The truth is that God wants you to experience freedom more than you want it. He loves to liberate souls through the power of Jesus' finished work. God hasn't promised us an easy life, a problem-free life or a temptation-free life, but He has promised us a new heart that desires to obey His commandments. In fact, God even promises us an *eXXXit* from every temptation in 1 Corinthians 10:13: "No temptation has overtaken you except such as is common to man; but God *is* faithful, who will not allow you to be tempted beyond what you are able, but with the temptation will also make the way of escape, that you may be able to bear *it*. " Open your heart to receive from God. He loves you so much. Allow Jesus to help you *eXXXit* pornography by entering into His grace and truth.

It's important to remember that we never come to a place where we don't need Jesus. As you walk in freedom and people read the story of your life, you will just point them back to the story of Jesus. Taking the *eXXXit* isn't about seeing how great we are but allowing people to see how great Jesus is. Below is a spoken word piece that I wrote as a rallying cry for those who no longer want to be slaves to pornography, but who want to live free in Christ.

eXXXit

Dear pornography
What beautiful photography
You twisted psychology
You once befriended me

eXXXit

Told me I could call you porn for short

You lulled me to sleep like a mother rocks a baby
Injected my soul and put me under a spiritual anesthesia, amnesia

But somehow it was so deceiving
I thought help I was receiving

You offered me power
But then you became my master
Sin never looked so good
As I was led to the slaughter
Like you got someone's daughter

And destroyed her innocence
For a generation of malcontents

Yea, you dress things up real nice
But no matter what you say
You are wrecking women in abusive slavery
As you deceive them into false glory

You're in the corner store, on the web and tv
You're even in the church
You once had a place in me
And it's escaping me, breaking me

To think that I gave you time, a dime
For this Crime
Against humanity
For lying vanity

You were my security

I wouldn't let you go
I couldn't let you down
I was afraid of losing you
Oh the irony of Stockholm syndrome
Feeling at home
With a blood sucking vulture

You got women to measure by you their value
So now they can be sold to
The highest bidder
No one considers
Them being abused, raped, and damaged
But airbrush and surgery create a false advantage
Cause the pain just doesn't go away
It's not reality, it's a play for crappy pay

And Porn, you even got men forsaking their legacy
Thinking their strength is sexuality
So the sons, brothers, husbands and fathers
Just start wrecking destinies
As their slaves to these fantasies

I know the story all the while, see
I gave you an inch and you took a mile
You have tainted the culture
Destroyed marriages
Caused children to be left fatherless

I gave you my youth
And you gave me guilt shame and death
Took away my breath

But at death's door
I was awakened

By the hand of a heart beating
Bleeding love

See porn, I'm actually writing to inform you that

I found the *eXXXit*
Or rather the *eXXXit* found me
Christ is the Exodus
From pain to porn to purity
Jesus is the WAY out

Some say a crutch
I've found Him to be a strong tower
He Surrounded me
And He founded me
Unbounded me

See you have been replaced porn
By the Resurrected Life
The way you led and I died
Was eye candy laced with cyanide

But my pain's been robbed
See the Gospel isn't just some bandaid job
On a soul that is hemorrhaging from immorality

My neural pathways were retraced
My rejection replaced

So pornography you're not so dear to me
And though you make money by the billions
And get clicked on by the hundreds of millions
I will tell my story of redemption

Because I can hear
The sound
Of the masses
Marching to the Master
Making the eXXXit

Signed in sincerity, this your dear enemy,
A sinner made saint

CHAPTER ONE

Sex is God's Great Idea

¹⁸Let your fountain be blessed, And rejoice with the wife of your youth. ¹⁹As a loving deer and a graceful doe, Let her breasts satisfy you at all times; And always be enraptured with her love. ²⁰For why should you, my son, be enraptured by an immoral woman, And be embraced in the arms of a seductress? (Proverbs 5:18–20)

³Let the husband render to his wife the affection due her, and likewise also the wife to her husband. ⁴The wife does not have authority over her own body, but the husband does. And likewise the husband does not have authority over his own body, but the wife does. ⁵Do not deprive one another except with consent for a time, that you may give yourselves to fasting and prayer; and come together again so that Satan does not tempt you because of your lack of self-control (1 Corinthians 7:3–5).

Eat, O friends! Drink, yes, drink deeply, O beloved ones! (Song of Solomon 5:1)

It might seem strange to start a book on freedom from pornography and sexual sin with a chapter on how wonderful sex is. This book is not a "don't have sex" kind of book. It is a "have sex in the right place at the right time" kind of book. God knew that the happy place for sex is in marriage. In a marriage covenant God not only allows for sex, He actually encourages it and rejoices over it!

Mark and Grace Driscoll, in their book *Real Marriage*, say that historically, humans have tended to view sex either as god or as gross; it is neither. Sex is a gift.[1] God invented sex and He knows how it works best. God wants to give you a great sex life. He designed sex for procreation, but as we see in the Scriptures above, He also created sex for pleasure. In Proverbs 5:19, God tells husbands explicitly to enjoy their wives' breasts at all times. Even a casual reading through the Song of Solomon reveals that God wants married couples to bring creativity, passion and romance to their sex lives.

You have a sexual drive in your body. God does not want you to shut down your sex drive; He wants you to manage it in a way that brings Him glory and honors your future spouse.[2] Sexual desire is a gift from God. Oftentimes you may have felt that it was more of a curse because it is so strong. God will empower you to manage this drive and keep yourself pure for your spouse.

WORTH THE WAIT

Growing up, did your parents ever make you finish your dinner before you could eat dessert? Did you ever practice really hard for something for a long period of time so you could win the big game or give an excellent performance? That's delaying pleasure. We have to delay pleasure all the time. Delaying pleasure for the right purpose actually causes us to enjoy obtaining our goal even more. People in our culture often freak out when we talk about teaching people to delay pleasure, like it will destroy people. Delaying sexual pleasure will actually make your sex life in marriage more fulfilling.

Once I became a teenager, one of my greatest fears was Jesus returning before I got to get married and have sex. In fact, that might be one of the greatest fears of most young men in the church, which is pretty funny looking back. If you wait to enjoy sex in marriage then you will enter marriage with a clean conscience and be so thankful to give yourself fully to your spouse.

After seeing the effects of those who choose to wait for marriage to have sex and those that don't, I can tell you that waiting is totally worth it. When I worked at a store while attending community college, a young lady I worked with approached me one day and with a mocking tone told me, "The only reason you don't have sex is because you don' t know what you are missing." She knew I was a Christian. I was stunned at the time and didn't know what to say to her. Now, having been married and having fathered four children, I see that I was not missing out. Research shows that multiple sexual partners and experiences can hurt your sex life in the future (more about that in the next chapter).

Ladies, just to let you know, guys *do* say things like, "Oh, her, she's the one you have sex with but not the kind you marry." Just giving yourself away before marriage doesn't do anything to help you get a good husband.

Young men, God is trusting you with His daughters. The young ladies that are in your life are someone else's daughters as well. Treat them well, like you would want someone to treat the girl that you marry one day.

Thankfully, God can do anything to heal and restore you if you are not sexually pure or if you have given yourself over to pornography. The reason I am talking about sex before marriage in a book about pornography is because they are totally related. Just looking at pornography before marriage is giving up the virginity of your heart and mind. It can open up the door to hooking up with real people as well.

Satan seeks to destroy people through immoral sexual experiences. He can make it appear so attractive and so enticing, but all he does is twist the beauty that God created. Sin perverts and destroys what God made as holy. So don't confuse the good blessings that God has made with the results of sin upon those blessings.

Sex inside of marriage is also a deterrent from sexual sin. Paul told the Corinthian church that husbands and wives should regularly have sex and that this would help them conquer sexual temptation. God loves sex. If He didn't want people to have sex, He wouldn't have made it so pleasurable. Sex feels great. It is a gift of God to husbands and wives. As a gift, sex should never be used as a threat or a demand. One spouse should not demand it whenever they want it and the other spouse should not withhold it whenever they want. I have heard sex in marriage often likened to a thermometer rather than a thermostat. This means that if the spark is missing in sex in a marriage, it usually means that something is going wrong in other areas. However, if sexual intimacy is fulfilling for both spouses and full of passion, that is usually a sign that other areas in the relationship are going well.

Many people desire to marry. There are very few who may feel a call to be celibate for life. The Bible calls celibacy a special gift. If you desire strongly to be married, you probably don't have the gift of celibacy. God said in Genesis 2:18, "And the LORD God said, "It is not good that man should be alone; I will make him a helper comparable to him." God didn't want us to be alone.

PORNOGRAPHY ENDANGERS MARRIAGE

It's important to realize that marriage will not fix you if you desire to look at pornography. Jesus takes away our sin, not our spouse. But it is also important to view sex as a special gift from God. You need to see sex in a positive light, as long as it is put in the proper context of covenant marriage love.

Pornography robs us of the proper view of sex. It treats sex like something that you consume only for your selfish pleasure. Sex is supposed to be a part of a relationship between a man and a woman who are committed to each other until death. As we will see in the next chapter, your sexual experiences bond your mind to that experience. When you repeatedly bond yourself to your spouse in sexual intimacy, you are creating a stronger bond in your marriage.

You might be a long way off from marriage. So, why am I telling you this? You might feel like "THIS IS NOT HELPING ME!" Well, you need to look forward to having sex and have a high value for it being reserved for marriage love.

The devil works as hard as he can to get you to have sex before you are married and to get involved in pornography. Then, once you are married, he will try to dull your desire for sex with your spouse. After you get married you still have to manage your sex drive and focus solely on your spouse. You honor God by obeying His instructions on sexuality. It is an act of worship to enjoy a sexual relationship with your husband or wife and to refrain from one while you are unmarried.

Pornography conditioned my mind to think that sex was something that was all about me, and it brought shame and hiding into my life. Even though I had been free from pornography for several years when I got married, it was like I had to remind myself for a while that this was not sinful, but actually a good thing to enjoy from God.

Marriage is a great blessing. It is important to let your identity be formed before you get married. Don't look for a marriage to solve your sexual issues or your self-image issues. If you are not yet married, look forward to marriage but start to develop and mature as a man or woman of God. Start to become someone who is ready to be married.

I want to give you a vision for God's purpose for sex. In Proverbs 29:18 we read "Where there is no revelation, the people cast off restraint; But happy is he who keeps the law." In other words, where you have no revelation or vision for your life, you have no boundaries and start to go crazy. But you will be happy if you live in God's law. God didn't make sex for marriage to make your single life miserable. He did it to bless your married life and keep you healthy while you are single as well.

Vision for a great sex life will cause you to temporarily delay pleasure in your life while you are single. Live with the end in mind. If you want a successful sex life, a lasting marriage, a healthy family and a legacy one day, then you will choose to look at sex as a positive thing that is worth the wait. Pornography and premarital sex will rob you of this vision. Every choice you make today will affect your future. The choices you make today are based on the vision you have. If you only think of the next five minutes, you can be led into some pretty stupid choices. But when you see things God's way, you are equipped to make choices that are the most helpful and happy for you.

Again, God made sex and wants you to enjoy it. So begin to follow His instructions. You will not regret obeying God in the end. His commandments are to bring us joy, not to be a rulebook that weighs us down (John 15:9-11). Ask God for His help to view sex through His eyes and thank Him that He has your best interest in mind.

CHAPTER TWO

Sin with a Capital "S"

> *15 Woe to him who gives drink to his neighbor, pressing him to your bottle, even to make him drunk, that you may look on his nakedness! 16 You are filled with shame instead of glory* (Habakkuk 2:15-16a).

> *18 Flee sexual immorality. Every sin that a man does is outside the body, but he who commits sexual immorality sins against his own body. 19 Or do you not know that your body is the temple of the Holy Spirit who is in you, whom you have from God, and you are not your own? 20 For you were bought at a price; therefore glorify God in your body and in your spirit, which are God's* (1 Corinthians 6:18-20).

Time and time again men and women are deceived into lies about sexuality. People often think that whatever they do sexually, as long as it is consented to by both parties, won't do them any harm. Others think that sexual sin might hurt them a little, but if they are looking at pornography and nobody else knows, it's not hurting anyone else. Both of these are lies. Sexual sin hurts all kinds of people; it is never a completely "private" sin.

I want you to know that if you are dealing with sexual sin and addictive behavior, you are not alone. This book is all about helping you get free in the knowledge that you are loved even in your sin and that Jesus can give you a brand new, pure heart.

In this chapter I want to expose what goes on in and through the pornography industry. I don't intend to bring shame on anyone for what they have done. I do believe that an important step in overcoming sexual sin is to see it for what it really is. I want to give you fuel to take the *eXXXit* out of porn.

In the second Scripture passage above we see the apostle Paul's ancient warning to the Corinthian church that sexual sin is unlike every other sin in that it affects the person who sins in this way with a larger consequence. All sin is outside the body except sexual sin, which is a sin against your own body. The Bible is clear that all sin is equal and equally able to be forgiven. So someone who commits sexual sin and someone who lies have both sinned against God. One is not worse than the other. God forgives both sins the same, through Jesus' finished work on the cross. Although God forgives sexual sin just as readily as any other sin, the consequences of it are not the same.

You are totally tied to your sexuality simply by existing. Think about it. When you are born, everyone wants to know *what* you are. Everyone asks your mom or dad, "Is it a boy or a girl?" That is a sexual statement. Your gender, male or female, is also known as your sex. Your sex is determined by what kind of body parts you are born with (and other factors too). As human beings we are sexual beings by creation. Our sexuality is part of who we are. That's not bad at all and shouldn't be embarrassing. It is just a reality of life. When we sin sexually, we sin against who we are. When we give ourselves over to sexual experiences that aren't according to the Bible, we face consequences for disobeying God's ways. However, just as the sin of breaking God's plan for sexuality can be forgiven, the consequences of that sin can be healed through the work of Jesus.

Pornography is a multi-billion dollar industry, but its cost to the moral and spiritual health of people is even greater. The effects of pornography and sexual sin are powerful and pervasive. Indeed, the statistics and effects are overwhelming:

PORNOGRAPHY STATISTICS[3]

- American children begin consuming hardcore pornography at an average age of 11.

- Four out of five 16-year-olds regularly access pornography online.

- The pornography industry is a $97 billion business worldwide.

- The pornography industry is a $13 billion business in the United States.

- Internet pornography in the United States is a $3 billion industry.

- Every second…
  - $3,075.64 is spent on pornography.
  - 28,258 Internet users are viewing pornography.
  - 372 Internet users are typing adult search terms into search engines.

- Every 39 minutes, a new pornographic video is made in the United States.

- One out of three youth who viewed pornography, viewed the pornography intentionally.

- Seven out of ten youth have accidentally come across pornography online.

- Nearly 80 percent of unwanted exposure to pornography is taking place in the home (79 percent occurs in the home; 9 percent occurs at school; 7 percent other/unknown; 5 percent at a friend's home).

- Kids experience unwanted exposure to sexual material via:
  - A link came up as a result of an innocent word search (40 percent)
  - Clicking on a link in another site (17 percent)
  - A pop-up (14 percent)
  - Other (13 percent)
  - Misspelled web address (12 percent)
  - Don't know (4 percent)

- Internet pornography was blamed for a 20 percent increase in sexual attacks by children over three years.

- Roughly two-thirds (67 percent) of young men and one-half (49 percent) of young women agree that viewing pornography is acceptable.

- Nearly 9 out of 10 (87 percent) young men and 1 out of 3 (31 percent) young women report using pornography.

- Experts have warned that the rise in the viewing of pornography was implicated in a variety of problems, including a rise in the levels of STDs and teenage pregnancies. Additionally, males aged between 12 and 17 who regularly viewed pornography had sex at an earlier stage in life and were more likely to initiate oral sex, apparently imitating what they had seen.

- Nearly 74 percent of pornography websites surveyed display adult content on their homepage (accessible to anyone) before asking if the viewers are of legal age.

PORNOGRAPHY EFFECTS ON BEHAVIOR

- "Teens who watch a lot of such sexualized programming are twice as likely to engage in sexual intercourse themselves."[4]

- "Causing 12 year old children to think pornographic behavior was normal, propelling many into copycat sexual actions and causing nightmares and other direct signs of anxiety."[5]

- "A recent study from the Centers for Disease Control and Prevention found that 'regular porn users are more likely to report depression and poor physical health than nonusers are. ... The reason is that porn may start a cycle of isolation. ... Porn may become a substitute for healthy face-to-face interactions, social or sexual'...Young men -- who play video games and use porn the most -- are being digitally rewired in a totally new way that demands constant stimulation. And those delicate, developing brains are being catered to by video games and porn-on-demand, with a click of the mouse, in endless variety. Such new brains are also totally out of sync in traditional school classes, which are analog, static and interactively passive...Guys are also totally out of sync in romantic relationships, which tend to build gradually and subtly, and require interaction, sharing, developing trust and suppression of lust at least until 'the time is right.'" [6]

PORNOGRAPHY EFFECTS ON THE BODY AND BRAIN

- Someone who has been involved in Internet pornography for an extended period of time has a brain that looks a lot like that of a cocaine addict.[7]

- According to Dr. William Struthers, men who use porn become controlling as well as highly introverted, have high anxiety, become narcissistic and curious, have low self-esteem, and become depressed, dissociative, and distractible. [8]

- "Ironically, while viewing porn creates momentary intensely pleasurable experiences, it ends up leading to several negative lingering psychological experiences. As men fall deeper into the mental habit of fixating on [pornographic images], the exposure to them creates neural pathways. Like a path is created in the woods with each successive hiker, so do the neural paths set the course for the next time an erotic image is viewed. Over time these neural paths become wider as they are repeatedly traveled with each exposure to pornography. They become the automatic pathway through which interactions with woman are routed.... They have unknowingly created a neurological circuit that imprisons their ability to see women rightly as created in God's image."[9]

- Writing in *New York Magazine*, Naomi Wolf observes, "[P]ornography works in the most basic of ways on the brain: It is Pavlovian. An orgasm is one of the biggest reinforcers imaginable. If you associate orgasm with your wife, a kiss, a scent, a body, that is what, over time, will turn you on; if you open your focus to an endless stream of ever-more-transgressive images of cybersex slaves, that is what it will take to turn you on. The ubiquity of sexual images does not free eros but dilutes it."[10]

- Pamela Paul, in her book *Pornified*, writes, "Pornography leaves men desensitized to both outrage and to excitement, leading to an overall diminishment of feeling and eventually to dissatisfaction with the emotional tugs of everyday life...Eventually they are left with a confusing mix of supersized expectations about sex and numbed emotions about women...When a man gets bored with pornography, both his fantasy and real worlds become imbued with indifference. The real world often gets really boring..."[11]

- At another place in the same book, Paul quotes a psychologist and pornography researcher at Texas A&M: "'Softcore pornography has a very negative effect on men as well. The problem with softcore pornography is that its voyeurism teaches men to view women as objects rather than to be in relationships with women as human beings.' According to Brooks, pornography gives men the false impression that sex and pleasure are entirely divorced from relationships. In other words, pornography is inherently self-centered–something a man does by himself, for himself–by using another woman as the means to pleasure, as yet another product to consume.[12]

- "In a hearing before the U.S. Senate Committee, Dr. Judith Reisman quoted neurologist Richard Restak: Thanks to the latest advances in neuroscience, we now know that pornographic visual images imprint and alter the brain, triggering an instant, involuntary, but lasting biochemical memory trail, arguably subverting the First Amendment by overriding the cognitive speech process. This is true of so-called 'soft-core' and 'hard-core' pornography. And once new neuro-chemical pathways are established they are difficult or impossible to delete.

  "Pornographic images also cause secretion of the body's 'fight or flight' sex hormones. This triggers excitatory transmitters and produces non-rational, involuntary reaction; intense arousal states that overlap sexual lust—now with fear, shame and/or hostility and violence. Media erotic fantasies become deeply imbedded, commonly coarsening, confusing, motivating and addicting many of those exposed. Pornography triggers myriad kinds of internal, natural drugs that mimic the 'high' from a street drug. Addiction to pornography is addiction to what I dub erototoxins—mind-altering drugs produced by the viewer's own brain.

  "How does this 'brain sabotage' occur? Brain scientists tell us that 'in 3/10 of a second a visual image passes from the eye through the brain, and whether or not one wants to, the brain is structurally changed and memories are created. We literally 'grow new brain' with each visual experience."[13]

DIVORCE AND PORNOGRAPHY STATISTICS

Daniel Weiss, writing for *Citizen Link*, a public policy partner of *Focus on the Family*, discussed the link between pornography and divorce, citing a survey of 350 attorneys attending a 2002 meeting of the American Academy of Matrimonial Lawyers. According to the survey, 62 percent said that the Internet played a significant role in the divorces of the past year; specifically, in 58% of marriages that ended, pornography was a significant factor.[14]

PORNOGRAPHY AND THE HUMAN TRAFFICKING LINK

In his book *Sexual Healing*, David Kyle Foster describes the insidious link between pornography and sex trafficking: "In even the most 'respected' girlie and boy magazines, there is an incredible amount of sexual abuse and exploitation going on behind the scenes. In the world of pornography, it is not unusual for young girls and boys to be kidnapped off the streets, force-fed addictive drugs and gang-raped in order to break down their resistance to being used. In some cases, they are brutally treated, tortured and even killed. They are often forced into prostitution. This goes on every day in every major city (and some towns) of this country. And the person who finances it is the person who buys pornography—you and me! Not only do we finance their practices, but our porn money is also used for other activities of organized crime, including murder, rape, prostitution, extortion, and who knows what else."[15]

STD STATISTICS

There is not enough room in this book to list STD statistics, but much information is available at www.cdc.gov/std. If you have been sexually active and made genital contact through any type of oral sex, anal sex or intercourse, you need to see a doctor as soon as possible to get tested for possible diseases. Some diseases show no visible signs in their early stages, and if they are caught early on there is a better chance for treatment. Be brave and get tested; it is the best thing you can do for your physical health if you are or have been sexually active.

CONCLUSION

Pornography and sexual sin affect everyone. We need to stop being ignorant to what we are facing and start to *eXXXit* this way of bondage. There is hope and healing for those who have been bound. This chapter is not intended to depress you but to arm you with information about what is really going on in and through the sex industry. My life is proof that you don't have to be controlled by your past. Keep reading! The truth that lies ahead in these next chapters will set you free because they are full of what Jesus has offered.

CHAPTER THREE

How Sexual
Sin Operates

Although the Bible is an ancient book, it is totally applicable to the issues that we face today. In the Book of Proverbs, Solomon writes about a young man who is seduced by a married woman who dresses and acts like a prostitute. This warning is not only a timeless warning to young men about the advances of women set on impure things; I believe it's a picture of how the spirit behind sexual sin operates to entrap people in its snare.

In this chapter we will go verse by verse to pull out meanings and applications that will help us walk in freedom and avoid the trap of pornography.

> *⁷My son, keep my words, And treasure my commands within you. ²Keep my commands and live, And my law as the apple of your eye. ³Bind them on your fingers; Write them on the tablet of your heart. ⁴Say to wisdom, "You are my sister," And call understanding your nearest kin, ⁵That they may keep you from the immoral woman, From the seductress who flatters with her words* (Proverbs 7:1-5).

Solomon states here that the number one thing we can do to stay away from the power of sexual sin is to keep God's law and God's wisdom as the main focus of our life. What he has in mind here is reading the Bible, memorizing it, focusing on it, meditating on it, etc. Note how he uses phrases such as, "treasure my commands," "keep my commands…as the apple of your eye," "bind them on your fingers," and "write them on the tablet of your heart." In other words, Solomon is telling us to let God's Word become deeply imbedded in our heart. When God's Word is in your heart your desire starts to change from longing for pornography to longing for God. He becomes your greatest desire.

THE FOOLISH YOUNG MAN

> *⁶For at the window of my house I looked through my lattice, ⁷And saw among the simple, I perceived among the youths, A young man devoid of understanding* (Proverbs 7:6-7).

One major problem I dealt with as a teenager was not knowing how to spend my time or who to spend it with. I would wander around and end up hanging out with people that were a horrible influence on me. When you are young, boredom is the one thing that you try and escape the most. I remember working in fast food when I was 16 and how my manager, Scott, used to say to me, "Idle hands are the devil's workshop." He meant that if you aren't doing anything good with your hands, the devil will give you something bad to do. One of the reasons I got into pornography early on was not because I wanted to sin but simply because I was bored and didn't understand what to do with my time.

Take it from me, you are heading for trouble if you start spending hours surfing the web for no reason, or channel surfing on TV endlessly, or looking for some other guys to hang out with, even if you know they are probably going to watch movies you shouldn't see or pull out their dad's porn collection. Maybe your mom or sister has fashion magazines or lingerie catalogs that come in the mail and you start acting without understanding for no other reason (initially) than that you are bored. These kinds of choices that seem so casual and harmless in the beginning can be an entry point for the evil of sexual temptation and sin.

> *⁸Passing along the street near her corner; And he took the path to her house ⁹In the twilight, in the evening, In the black and dark night* (Proverbs 7:8-9).

It's interesting that this young man was out at night. Night speaks of the hidden things in our lives. Whether it's at night or during the day, people are deceived in the belief that pornography is a secret that only affects them. This is absolutely untrue. Pornography affects you, God, your family, your church, your job, your present or future wife or husband, your present or future children, and your friendships. It might start in the dark, but if you choose to go down this path it will severely damage every area of your life.

THE CRAFTY HARLOT

> *¹⁰And there a woman met him, With the attire of a harlot, and a crafty heart. ¹¹She was loud and rebellious, Her feet would not stay at home. ¹²At times she was outside, at times in the open square, Lurking at every corner. ¹³So she caught him and kissed him; With an impudent face she said to him:* (Proverbs 7:10-13).

We see here how aggressive this woman is by the way she dresses, the way she uses her loud voice and the way she forces herself on this young man. Sexual immorality is an aggressive thing. Sexual images are all over the place. I don't care if you are homeschooled or go to Christian school; if you have a computer or a TV in your house, the truth is you will be exposed to sexual advertising and to people who walk in sexually impure ways. It's almost impossible to do something as simple as buy gum at a convenience store without being bombarded with sexual images from magazines at the checkout stand. You don't have to try hard to look for ways to sin sexually. That's why it is important to be on your guard continually. Sexual sin will try and hunt you down and make you feel like there is no way out. Of course, that isn't true; there is ALWAYS a way out, and God wants to give you confidence. Just remember that this sexual stuff is forceful and doesn't play by the rules.

> [14] *"I have peace offerings with me; Today I have paid my vows"* (Proverbs 7:14).

Sexual sin always has a spirit of compromise behind it. This woman told the young man that she had given her offerings to God. Sexual sin doesn't care if you have a little bit of religion or spirituality in your life. The devil wants you to have a mixture: righteousness *and* sinfulness; godliness *and* worldliness.

When I was a youth pastor it always amazed me to watch how God would do a great work in a young person's life and then the devil would bring about a great distraction. Let's say a young lady gives her life to Jesus and starts a passionate relationship with God. Well, shortly after this happens, a guy enters that young lady's life who wants to date her but is not a Christian and does not share her godly values. He says things like, "I think I might want to be a Christian," or, "I'm not a Christian but I think it's great that you are." Slowly his influence draws her away from church and away from loving Jesus.

This is a false front to get you to hook up and compromise your purity. Sexual sin makes false promises to allure you into its trap. It encourages you to go to church and do all the right outward things, but continue to give your heart to immorality. Be careful, young people, of those who would deceive you to believe that you can still follow God even while you live in sexual impurity.

THE POWER OF SEDUCTION

> *[15]"So I came out to meet you, Diligently to seek your face, And I have found you. [16]I have spread my bed with tapestry, Colored coverings of Egyptian linen. [17]I have perfumed my bed With myrrh, aloes, and cinnamon. [18]Come, let us take our fill of love until morning; Let us delight ourselves with love"* (Proverbs 7:15-18).

We see again how sexual sin tries to allure people. Sexual sin appears to be so beautiful, passionate and romantic. Sin is fun for a season but no matter how things get dressed up, sexual sin causes much heartache and destruction. As we read in chapter two, there really is no one who wins from a life of sexual immorality.

> *[19]"For my husband is not at home; He has gone on a long journey; [20] He has taken a bag of money with him, And will come home on the appointed day"* (Proverbs 7:19-20).

Sexual sin will lie to you that there are no consequences or that there will be delayed consequences. You will hear things like, "You are so young." "You don't need to worry, no one will find out." "This doesn't affect anyone but you." "You can always stop this when you get married." "You are not hurting anyone." These are all outright lies. Sexual sin carries many consequences. The devil's strategy is to tell you that everyone does it and it doesn't hurt people. He wants you to think that everything will be okay while you live in compromise. Again, as we read earlier, there are horrible consequences to your relationships, your mind, and your body. Your sin will find you out (Numbers 32:23) At one point or another you will face consequences.

> *[21]With her enticing speech she caused him to yield, With her flattering lips she seduced him* (Proverbs 7:21).

49

Sexual sin tells you what you want to hear. It deceives you by making you think that you are powerful and beautiful for the wrong reasons. You are powerful and beautiful because you are made in the image of God. Sexuality does not give you value. God will affirm you as His son or daughter. Sexual sin cries out from the media, "How to be sexy." "How to become more desirable." Be careful of the words that romance your heart. Insecurity will allow sexual sin to get a foothold in your life. When you are secure about who you are in Christ, then the devil's words over you hold no power. But when you don't know who you are, then anyone who says flattering things over you can set you up to be manipulated and controlled by the world's system and its master, the devil.

THE DESTRUCTIVENESS OF SEXUAL SIN

> [22]*Immediately he went after her, as an ox goes to the slaughter, Or as a fool to the correction of the stocks* (Proverbs 7:22).

Sexual sin offers you a feeling of power, worth and beauty. But in reality it is leading you to the slaughter, where you become powerless and feel worthless and ugly. On the outside sexual sin looks very attractive and appealing, but it relentlessly destroys marriages as one of the leading causes of divorce. It causes people to contract sexually transmitted diseases that may lead to premature death. It creates sexual dysfunction by preventing married couples from enjoying their sex lives. Pornography leads women to compare themselves to others, resulting in self-hatred when they feel they don't measure up to others. At the same time, pornography fuels men to treat women with contempt and even hatred. The good news is that Jesus was a "lamb led to the slaughter" (Is. 53:7) so that we don't have to be slaughtered. Jesus was sacrificed for our sin so that we could be forgiven and avoid the destruction that sin brings.

> *²³Till an arrow struck his liver. As a bird hastens to the snare, He did not know it would cost his life* (Proverbs 7:23).

Here Solomon reminds us that sexual sin not only affects our spiritual and emotional health but also our physical health. Even back in Bible days people were able to observe how sexual sin brought about physical destruction. If it was true back then it is even truer today. Sexually transmitted infections and diseases continue to increase and adapt, causing more and more problems for those who practice sexual sin.

Sometimes people believe the lie that the medical community will invent cures by the time they get a disease. Thank God for great medical breakthroughs, but as diseases evolve they can start resisting medical solutions that used to work. God can heal you, and there are cures and helps for some sexual diseases. But many remain unresolved, and viruses will stay with you for life unless you receive a miracle. Don't test God in this area by playing around with sexual sin as though nothing is going to happen to you. If you have been sexually active in any way that includes genital contact, you need to get tested for sexual diseases and infections right away. The earlier you catch something, the better it is. Sexual diseases can be hidden and not show symptoms at first. It is critical that you get tested right away even if you don't feel sick or feel like you have any symptoms. Call someone today to go with you if you need support. Call today and get a doctor's appointment. God will be with you; do not be afraid.

> *²⁴Now therefore, listen to me, my children; Pay attention to the words of my mouth: ²⁵Do not let your heart turn aside to her ways, Do not stray into her paths; ²⁶For she has cast down many wounded, And all who were slain by her were strong men* (Proverbs 7:24-26).

It is interesting that all who were slain by her were "strong men." We need to learn to be vulnerable and transparent about our temptations and our failings in sin. Pretending to have it all together when you don't will trip you up in sexual sin. God promised the apostle Paul in 2 Corinthians 12:9 that His strength would be made perfect in Paul's weakness. Being weak is not about being defeated. Being weak before God has to do with humility and dependency upon God. Don't become arrogant and think that you can defeat sexual sin without God's help or without the help of other brothers and sisters in Christ. Be humble.

> [27]*Her house is the way to hell, Descending to the chambers of death* (Proverbs 7:27).

Finally, we see the end of a life that will not turn to God but continues in sexual sin: eternal death, torment and separation from God.

PRAYER OF REPENTANCE AND FAITH

Sexual sin is really a small part of a larger problem. It stems from the root of sin, which keeps man separate from God and not dependent upon God for salvation. Ultimately, the greatest sin is rejecting the sacrifice of Jesus for your forgiveness. Not believing in Jesus and His work on the cross for you is what keeps you from heaven. However, if you have received Jesus and His free gift of salvation, your heart has been transformed and you have become a new creature who should not want sexual sin, or any other sin for that matter. God did not send Jesus to condemn the world but to save it (John 3:17). If you don't think that you have received this gift of God and that you have eternal life, you can ask God to forgive you right now. The truth is that Jesus paid for your sin and experienced death so that you don't have to. God does not want anyone to go to hell but for all to receive new life. If you desire to have peace with God, where you don't have to fear hell, where you have eternal hope and a new heart to follow God, then pray this prayer right now:

Father God, thank you for sending Jesus to suffer and die in my place. I admit that I am a sinner. I have done many things wrong against you and others. I admit my weaknesses and failures to you. (Take time to name specific things that you feel guilty for). I believe that Jesus died for me on the cross and rose from the dead. I ask you now to be my Lord and Savior. Come and give me a new heart. Take away all my sin and shame. Cleanse me from all unrighteousness. Thank you that you love me and that you forgive me. Thank you for cleansing me and taking all my guilt away. Show me how to live a new life in Christ. Fill me up and empower me, Holy Spirit, to live a life after God. Consume me with a passion for Jesus. Consume me with a desire for holiness. Thank you, God, for saving me and giving me new life. In Jesus' name, Amen.

Through faith in Jesus you are a new creature. You are born again. Praise God! He has forgiven you of your sin and made you a new person.

CHAPTER FOUR

Light Walker

⁵This is the message which we have heard from Him and declare to you, that God is light and in Him is no darkness at all. ⁶If we say that we have fellowship with Him, and walk in darkness, we lie and do not practice the truth. ⁷But if we walk in the light as He is in the light, we have fellowship with one another, and the blood of Jesus Christ His Son cleanses us from all sin (1 John 1:5-7).

I remember moments growing up when I was determined to be open about my sinful struggle with pornography. I would gain a little momentum of confidence and think that I actually had the courage to talk to my dad or another man that I could trust. I would be right on the edge of confession and then suddenly an overwhelming sense of shame would grip my heart. I would have thoughts like, "You can't tell anyone; they will think you are a pervert. Nobody is doing this stuff." I later learned this was the same lying voice that was telling me, "It's okay to look at pornography. Everyone else is doing it. It's just a normal thing for a guy to do."

In hindsight I see the contradiction of these lies. On the one hand I believed I was all-alone and no one was as gross as me, but on the other I believed everybody my age was doing it. The devil just picked whatever lie would fit the moment to keep me bound.

Transparency is the greatest initial weapon that you have in your battle with pornography and your *eXXXit* into freedom. The apostle John was writing as we see above about the power of walking in the light and coming out of darkness. The darkness in 1 John 1 represents a life that is hiding its sin and issues. Sin grows in the dark. Warren Buffet once said, "Chains of habit are too light to be felt until they are too heavy to be broken." Whatever sin we hide from God becomes a stronger and stronger chain over time. Sin gives the allure of power but then it dominates. You are usually tempted to sin in small ways first, and hide that small thing in the darkness. But pretty soon that small thing starts to have a life of its own and goes from wanting a little to demanding all of your heart.

Hopefully by now you realize that it is very dangerous to walk in the darkness of pornography. Pornography is certainly very dark, as we have seen in the previous chapters. Unless you recognize the darkness of pornography, there is really no way to get out of it. You need to begin to hate this darkness so that you want nothing to do with it (*not* hate yourself; there is a big difference).

BE HUMBLE

How do you deal with darkness? You turn the light on. When you are in your room and you can't find something while it's dark in the middle of the night, what do you do to find it? Flip the switch so the light comes on. You must begin to bring this sin of pornography out of hiding in your life. You must become transparent. If you don't hate the sin more then you like the comfort of having a secret world then you probably won't deal with it. But if you don't care if you have to humble yourself and open up about your sin because it will bring you freedom, you are on the path to victory.

First Peter 5:5 says, "Likewise you younger people, submit yourselves to your elders. Yes, all of you be submissive to one another, and be clothed with humility, for 'God resists the proud, But gives grace to the humble." Choosing to be transparent and walk in the light will cost you something. It will cost you your pride. But God promises His grace to those who humble themselves. If you want freedom, you need the grace of God. The way you access that grace is by humbling yourself. There is no other way around this principle.

I grew up in a Christian school where we always took time in class for prayer. The number one prayer request in my entire middle school and high school career was an "unspoken." The teacher would ask the class, "Does anyone have a prayer request?" A few students would raise their hands, and usually over half would respond with, "I have an unspoken request." This really meant that they didn't want anyone in their business. I don't think anyone's life has been transformed through unspoken requests. It's not bad to get prayer for general things, but when we open up specifically about what is going wrong in our lives, then there is power present to change by the grace of God.

BE HONEST

The first time that I started to really open up about my sin with my dad, I only cracked the door open on the truth. I didn't want to tell him everything because I thought he might blow up. I was still too worried about what other people thought. It took me a few months to start to be fully honest about what I had done with this lustful sin. I had to keep coming back and confessing, "Remember that last thing I told you? It really happened, but there was more. I didn't do that once; I did that three times." Or, "I didn't just struggle with that, I struggled with this too." It was better that I started opening up a little bit, but I needed to learn to be fully honest. Then, after I started being honest, I didn't get a reaction of anger. I started realizing, "I should have done this a long time ago."

Walking in the light starts with being fully honest before God. The Bible is clear that we don't need a man to go between God and us because Jesus is our go between, He is our High Priest (Hebrew 4:14-16). God knows everything that we have done whether it is good, bad or ugly. But he wants us to humble ourselves before Him and tell Him anyway. It is so powerful to release your burdens to God. You can cast all your cares on Him because He cares for you (1 Peter 5:7). God wants to hear about your desire to be free and to hear you confess all of your sin.

CONFESS YOUR SIN

In 1 John 1:8-9 we read, "If we say that we have no sin, we deceive ourselves. If we confess our sins, He is faithful and just to forgive us our sins and to cleanse us from all unrighteousness." When we come to the point where we realize the darkness we have been in—when we realize our sin—then we must begin to confess it to God. This is how we become transparent and take the *eXXXit*. We own up to our choices that have displeased God. To confess our sin means to say the same thing about our sin that God does. We are not only supposed to admit what we have done but admit that it is totally wrong. We are not supposed to make excuses.

When I was a junior high pastor I had a student come to me and open up about his struggle with pornography. He brought it out of darkness and into the light. I prayed a simple prayer with him that day. He has come back to me over five years later and said that he has never struggled with pornography since we prayed that prayer that day. For him, the greatest breakthrough came just by this simple truth of bringing hidden things to the light. Again, the promise is that "in the light" we have the "blood of Jesus that cleanses us from all sin."

The first person to talk to about your sin is God. He is the One who is ready to help you and set you free. However, the next part of walking in the light has to do with opening up before others. God has called us to live in Christian community as believers, and we can't defeat things in our own strength. Transparency before God should always lead us to transparency with others. Sometimes people think it's either/or, like having to choose between God or someone else. But the Bible teaches both very clearly. So do both.

James 5:16a states, "Confess your trespasses to one another, and pray for one another, that you may be healed." When we confess our sin to others and pray for each other, we get healed. The power of walking in the light promises cleansing and healing. Choose to live a life without secrets. I don't share my junk with all my friends or with everyone I meet, but I have someone that I can share my junk with (several people, actually). One of my mentors, John Fuller, passed on some valuable wisdom to me when he said, "Globalize your success and localize your failures." What he meant was to tell everyone about things that are going good in your life but only tell a few people about your sin and your problems. You don't have to tell everyone about the sin in your life, but you should talk to someone.

How do you choose someone to confess sin to? I would pick someone who is more mature in their relationship with Jesus than you are, such as a parent, a spouse, a pastor, a teacher, a counselor or a mentor. I would not look for someone to be open with who is currently struggling with a porn addiction. Nor would I pick someone of the opposite sex. The idea is to find someone who is loving and Christ-like but who won't let you get away with sin without speaking truth into your life. It is also very helpful to have a group or to have more than one person you can speak openly with.

Walking in the light is the safest—and the most dangerous—jump of your life. Pornography tries to dominate your life by becoming a secret identity. You will start to break the back of pornography when you take it out of the secret darkness and into God's powerful light. I remember how much courage it took to step out and really start to live an open life. If you have already been actively involved in pornography, then your whole mindset up until this point is likely totally contrary to being open. That's not to give you an excuse. God will be with you to give you grace as you decide to humble yourself and obey Him in this area.

You need the power of God that is available through the cross. Jesus has paid for everything that you need to be free. Walking in the light positions you to receive all that the power of the cross has purchased for you. In the next chapter we will look at the power of the cross. It's time to *eXXXit* the darkness and enter God's glorious light!

Action Steps

1. Do you ever talk to God openly about your sin, your failures, your dreams or the deep things of your heart?

2. Spend some time alone with God and start to share with Him out loud the things that have been going on in your life.

3. Do you currently have a person or a group of people that you can share openly with about your sin, your failures, your dreams and the deep things of your heart?

4. Make a list of those people. (If you don't have anyone yet, make a list of those you would feel most comfortable approaching about pornography or the deep things going on in your heart.)

5. Call, text or set up a time to meet at least one person on your list right now or as soon as possible.

CHAPTER FIVE

The Power of the Cross

*²⁰And by Him to reconcile all things to Himself,
by Him, whether things on earth or things in heaven,
having made peace through the blood of His cross
(Colossians 1:20).*

*¹³And you, being dead in your trespasses and the un-
circumcision of your flesh, He has made alive together with
Him, having forgiven you all trespasses, ¹⁴having wiped
out the handwriting of requirements that was against us,
which was contrary to us. And He has taken it out of
the way, having nailed it to the cross. ¹⁵Having disarmed
principalities and powers, He made a public spectacle of
them, triumphing over them in it (Colossians 2:13-15).*

*²⁰I have been crucified with Christ; it is no longer
I who live, but Christ lives in me; and the life which I
now live in the flesh I live by faith in the Son of God,
who loved me and gave Himself for me. ²¹I do not set
aside the grace of God; for if righteousness comes through
the law, then Christ died in vain (Galatians 2:20-21).*

The reason you can porn-proof your life, be forgiven of all your sin and live a life of purity is all because of the cross. God loves you so much that while you were a sinner He sent His Son Jesus to die for you (Romans 5:8). The cross is the eternal evidence of God's love for you. God the Father sacrificed His Son for you on the worst day of your life. Jesus died for you on the day that you committed your worst sin. People often think that God loves them when they decide to get their act together or decide to go to church or decide to start being a good person. The gospel of Jesus Christ declares that God's love is so backwards (in the best possible way) to the love of the world. Others typically love us because of what we do for them. God loves us because "God is love" (1 John 4:8). God's love is based upon who He is, not upon what we have done. Paul says in Romans 5:10 that "when we were enemies we were reconciled to God through the death of His Son." This is the measuring stick of God's love: the cross. The death of Jesus permanently proves the love of God for us. God's love doesn't change for you based upon your performance.

"Performance" Doesn't Work

This is one of the greatest obstacles that I had to battle in overcoming the shame of pornography. I hated myself and I always tried to earn acceptance through how I performed. If I did great in sports or school, I felt great. When I outperformed others in grades or competitions, I was on top of the world. But when I was the worst on the team or others outshined me, I was in the pits. It is common for people who deal with a pornography addiction to have performance issues. The cross strikes to the heart of this issue. You CANNOT do anything to earn the love of God. You can't perform well enough to make God love you. He loves you and He proved it through the cross. The most popular verse in every children's church program is usually John 3:16: "For God so love the world that He gave His only begotten Son, that whoever believes in Him should not perish but have everlasting life." Right here we see that because God loves, He gives. The greatness of His gift, His Son's death on the cross, is the sign of the greatness of His love.

If you don't see God and yourself in light of the cross it will not be possible to defeat the power of pornography or any other sin in your life. In Galatians, Paul taught very clearly that the only thing God's law (His rules) can do is show people how sinful they are. When you read the Bible and all you see is requirements that you keep on breaking all the time, you are only getting part of the picture. As Paul said in Galatians 2:21, "If righteousness comes through the law, then Christ died in vain." In other words, you can't become righteous or clean by doing good things. It is all (and only) through the cross of Jesus Christ that you can be forgiven and free. When you feel overwhelmed by God's requirements in the Bible, you need to remember that Jesus fulfilled all of those requirements for you and died in your place so that you can rejoice in what Jesus has done.

If you have desired to be free from the power of pornography for more than a few days, you have probably realized how just trying harder doesn't work at all. It might work for a couple of days or a couple of weeks, but you end up falling flat on your face. You can try and read the Bible more, schedule every minute of your day and put stickers on your TV screens that say "pure eyes" or "Jesus is watching you." You can even literally trash your computers or add accountability software. You can pray for 8 hours a day. Some of these things aren't bad to do at all, and you might need to do some of them, but if all you do is try and keep God's rules in your own strength, you are bound to fail miserably. You have to come to understand the power of God's love through the cross. If you aren't familiar with love then you aren't familiar with God. God's very essence is love. He not only does loving things or communicates His love; He is, in fact, love.

If you look at pornography today, you need to remember that God loves you. Your sin does not stop God from loving you. His love is what will change you. As long as you feel like you are striving in your own strength to stop sinning and please God, you are living under the law. You believe that by doing the right thing, you can earn something from God.

THE BLOOD OF JESUS IS ENOUGH

I had a breakthrough in my life one day in a conversation with my dad. I hadn't looked at pornography in several years. My behavior had totally changed, but I still faced so much shame. I always thought that my shame would not go away until I figured out just the right way to repent. Inside I felt that something was still deeply wrong with me, and until I could find this missing puzzle piece to my problem, God wouldn't really love me or accept me. In the middle of this conversation my dad asked, "John, do you think that the blood of Jesus is enough for you to be forgiven or do you think that you still have to do something else?"

The conversation had gotten to a pretty emotional place at this point, and a lie that I had believed for so long was squeezed right out of me. "There's got to be something else," I replied. I instantly hung my head, ashamed of what I had just spoken. I actually didn't believe that the blood of Jesus was enough for me to be loved by God and forgiven. I thought there was something more out there for me to do to gain God's acceptance. I instantly recanted my words but struggled to figure out what to do next. In the end there was nothing else I could do but embrace the love of God because of Jesus' shed blood on the cross. That day was a turning point for me. Once God uncovered that lie, He helped me change my mindset and I began experiencing His love. His love was already available to me even before I could figure it out. Today God's love is available to you too, even if you don't have everything figured out.

THE CROSS RECONCILES US TO GOD

So let's look at what happened on the cross. Col 1:20 says, "and by Him to reconcile all things to Himself, by Him, whether things on earth or things in heaven, having made peace through the blood of His cross." The cross of Jesus reconciled all things. Jesus made a payment with His blood on the cross that makes it possible for all people to be free from the dominating power of sin. Sin entered the world through Adam and is continually perpetuated by everyone born after Him. Romans 5:19 says, "For as by one man's disobedience many were made sinners, so also by one Man's obedience many will be made righteous." Man could not atone for His own sins. As stated earlier, the only thing the law did successfully was show us that we don't measure up to God's standard of perfection. It is through the obedience of Jesus, His obedience to the brutal death on the cross that allows us to have peace with God and become righteous.

The cross is the place of the great exchange. 2 Corinthians 5:21 says, "For He made Him who knew no sin to be sin for us, that we might become the righteousness of God in Him." On the cross, Jesus was made sin for us. He became our sin. God did this to make us become the righteousness of God. Think about how amazing this exchange is. Because of the cross, Jesus took upon Himself all of the judgment that we deserve and we get to receive all of the goodness that Jesus deserves. On the cross, Jesus experienced rejection so we could have acceptance with God. He experienced our pain so we could receive healing. He experienced our curse so that we could be blessed. He experienced the death that we deserve so that we could receive new life. Jesus became our pornography so we could live in freedom. Jesus became our sexual sin so that we could walk in purity.

Man's greatest need is to have peace with God and to experience God's love. If you are reading this and you haven't had your sins forgiven or you don't know if you have peace with God yet, today you can come to the cross of Jesus and enter into the greatest experience of your life. If you didn't yet take time to pray this prayer from Chapter 3, here it is again:

> Father God, thank you for sending Jesus to suffer and die in my place. I admit that I am a sinner. I have done many things wrong against you and others. I admit my weaknesses and failures to you (Take time to name specific things that you feel guilty for). I believe that Jesus died for me on the cross and rose from the dead. I ask you now to be my Lord and

Savior. Come and give me a new heart. Take away all my sin and shame. Cleanse me from all unrighteousness. Thank you that you love me and that you forgive me. Thank you for cleansing me and taking all my guilt away. Show me how to live a new life in Christ. Fill me up and empower me, Holy Spirit, to live a life after God. Consume me with a passion for Jesus. Consume me with a desire for holiness. Thank you, God, for saving me and giving me new life. In Jesus' name, Amen.

Through faith in Jesus you are a new creature. You are born again. Praise God! He has forgiven you of your sin and made you a new person.

ACTION STEP

1. Spend some time meditating on God's love and thanking God for how much He loves you because of the cross of Jesus Christ.

2. Ask God to reveal to you any ways that you are trying to earn His love in your own strength. Pray about this and share these revelations with those closest to you as you practice walking in the light.

CHAPTER SIX

Identification

¹⁷Therefore, if anyone is in Christ, he is a new creation; old things have passed away; behold, all things have become new (2 Corinthians 5:17).

⁴Therefore we were buried with Him through baptism into death, that just as Christ was raised from the dead by the glory of the Father, even so we also should walk in newness of life. ⁵For if we have been united together in the likeness of His death, certainly we also shall be in the likeness of His resurrection, ⁶knowing this, that our old man was crucified with Him, that the body of sin might be done away with, that we should no longer be slaves of sin. ⁷ For he who has died has been freed from sin (Romans 6:4-7).

The message of Christianity—the message of the gospel—is wilder than any other message on the planet. When you believe in what Jesus has done for you, you become BRAND NEW. Psalm 102:18 says, "This will be written for the generation to come, That a people yet to be created may praise the Lord."

The phrase "That a people yet to be created may praise the Lord" is a prophetic statement about people who would one day believe in Jesus. It's a statement about those who trust in Christ and become a brand new creation. When you come into faith in Jesus Christ you are not a sinner anymore. If you were an addict, you are not an addict anymore. If you were a pornographer, you are not a pornographer anymore. You become a new creature.

When you read through the New Testament you do not see things addressed to the sinners, the addicts or the perverts. You see things addressed to saints, to sons of God, to the church and to children of God. I'm not saying that Christians can't struggle with sin. I'm talking about your identity here. Do you see yourself as a sinner who is trying to earn a place in God's kingdom? Or do you see yourself as a child of God who is accepted because of the price that Jesus has paid for you?

The devil, the great enemy of our souls, is working overtime to get us to embrace the improper view of God and the wrong view of ourselves. This is the greatest case of identity theft on the planet. If the devil can make you identify with your sin and attach your value to shame, then you will continue to live out the way you see yourself. If you see yourself as a partier, you will party. If you see yourself as a drunk, you will go get drunk. If you see yourself as a pervert, you will stay bound in pornography. If you see yourself as powerless, you will always let people dominate you. Proverbs 23:7 states, "For as he thinks in his heart, so is he." In other words, the way you see yourself is the way that you will live. What you believe, you do. What you identify with becomes your reality.

The devil, your flesh and the world around you will try and pin you in a box that says you are stuck in this place forever. They will scream loudly that you are going to be a pervert for life and the best you can do is manage your sexual addiction. However, through the work of Jesus, you are offered the *eXXit*, a chance to end your old way of life and start over brand new. Identifying with what Jesus has done for you is a critical place for removing shame and guilt from your life.

Water baptism is an outward picture for Christians of the inner reality that occurs when we put our trust in Jesus. Romans 6 teaches that our baptism is a point of identification with the death, burial and resurrection of Jesus. In verse 6, we have this promise: "knowing this, that our old man was crucified with Him, that the body of sin might be done away with, that we should no longer be slaves of sin." You might believe that Jesus in a general sense has paid for your sin to get you to heaven one day. That is true; if you believe in Jesus and His payment for your sin, you will have heaven, but God paid for more than that. God paid for you to be free from sin in this life.

DEAD TO SIN BUT ALIVE TO GOD

Later in the same chapter Paul says:

> [11]*Likewise you also, reckon yourselves to be dead in-deed to sin, but alive to God in Christ Jesus our Lord.*
> [12]*Therefore do not let sin reign in your mortal body, that you should obey it in its lusts.* [13]*And do not present your members as instruments of unrighteousness to sin, but present yourselves to God as being alive form the dead, and your members as instruments of righteousness to God.* [14]*For sin shall not have dominion over you, for you are not under law but under grace* (Romans 6:11-14).

Paul's term "reckon" in verse 11 is an accounting term. It means to count. Our job is to take what Jesus has done and account for it. If I deposited $1 million in your checking account, it does not do you any good if you never access that account. Everyone who puts their faith in Jesus and passes from death to life has the righteousness of Jesus put into their account. But we need to access that deposit that Jesus has made by identifying that we died with Jesus and that we live new life because of His resurrection. By Jesus defeating the underlying root of sin in our lives, we are able to "not let sin reign in [our] mortal body."

The Bible is clear that water baptism is not what cleans our heart from sin; only the blood of Jesus can cleanse us from sin. First Peter

3:21 affirms this: "There is also an antitype which now saves us—baptism (not the removal of the filth of the flesh, but the answer of a good conscience toward God), through the resurrection of Jesus Christ." The blood of Jesus removes the filthiness of the flesh from us, but baptism gives us a good conscience because of the resurrection of Jesus Christ. There is nothing we can do to cleanse our guilty conscience. It is only what Jesus has done for us that can give us a clean conscience.

No Condemnation in Christ

Whenever we identify with our old way of life as a sinner, we put back on ourselves the very shame and condemnation that Jesus died to take away from us. Romans 8:1 declares, "There is therefore no condemnation to those who are in Christ Jesus, who do not walk according to the flesh, but according to the Spirit." When you identify that Jesus took all your punishment for all your sin upon Himself, condemnation loses its hold in your life. As I shared in the last chapter, I kept thinking I had to "do" something else to have this sense of shame removed from my life. But it was the issue of identification. I was still identifying with my past life that Jesus had put to death. If you focus on managing your past you will spend the rest of your life trying and failing to clean up your own mess. But when you embrace your value in Christ by identifying with Jesus, you can walk in freedom.

God has wired us with a conscience so that whenever we sin we experience a feeling of guilt associated with our wrong behavior. Guilt is a helpful teacher in our conscience to show us that we are violating boundaries that are healthy for us. Our conscience is a gift from God to monitor what is right or wrong. It is not always reliable, however, because our conscience can become twisted and defiled by repeated sin and shame. As Christians, if we continue to sin with pornography, we don't need to restore our own conscience. We need to return to the place of trusting the power of Jesus' blood shed for us on the cross. Hebrews 10:22 says, "Let us draw near with a true heart in full assurance of faith, having our hearts sprinkled from an evil conscience and our bodies washed with pure water." Our hearts are sprinkled by the blood of Jesus, and this is what cleans our conscience. Hebrews 9:14 assures us that "the blood of Christ... [cleanses our] conscience from dead works."

IDENTIFYING WITH CHRIST'S RIGHTEOUSNESS

Jesus identified with our sin so that we could identify with His righteousness. How do you see yourself? Do you see yourself as loved? You *are* loved. Do you see yourself as having value before God? You *do* have value. Identification has to do with taking the exchange of the cross and making it a part of your mindset. Here are some promises (this is not an exhaustive list) for you to begin to identify with because you are in Christ:

* I have authority over all the power of the enemy (Luke 10:19)

* I am loved by God (John 3:16)

* I have been set free by the Truth (John 8:31-32)

* I am held in my Father God's hand and no one can snatch me away (John 10:29)

* I am dead to sin (Romans 6:2-11)

* Sin shall not be master over me (Romans 6:14)

* I am not under condemnation (Romans 8:1)

* I am a child of God (Romans 8:16)

* I am more than a conqueror through Jesus who loves me (Romans 8:37)

* I am loved by Jesus (Romans 8:38-39)

* My body is a temple of the Holy Spirit (1 Corinthians 6:19)

* I was bought at a price (1 Corinthians 6:20)

* I am in Christ (2 Corinthians 5:17)

* I am a new creation (2 Corinthians 5:17)

* I am redeemed (Galatians 3:13)

* I have been crucified to the world and the world crucified to me (Galatians 6:14)

* I have been adopted, chosen and accepted by Father God (Ephesians 1:3-6)

* I have redemption through Christ's blood, and the forgiveness of sins (Ephesians 1:7)

* I have an inheritance in Christ (Ephesians 1:11)

* I have been sealed with the Holy Spirit of promise (Ephesians 1:13-14)

* I have been made alive together with Christ (Ephesians 2:4-5)

* I have been saved by grace through faith and not by works (Ephesians 2:8-9)

* I am God's workmanship (Ephesians 2:10)

* I am a citizen of heaven (Philippians 3:20)

* I am in the kingdom of the Son of God's love (Colossians 1:13)

* I am out of the kingdom of darkness (Colossians 1:13)

* Christ is in me, the hope of glory (Colossians 1:27)

* I have been made alive together with Jesus and forgiven of all my trespasses (Colossians 2:13)

* I have been raised with Christ (Colossians 3:3)

* I am the elect of God, holy and beloved (Colossians 3:12)

* I have not been given a spirit of fear, but of power, love and a sound mind (2 Timothy 1:7)

* My conscience is cleansed by the blood of Jesus (Hebrews 9:14)

ACTION STEP

1. Use this list of "Who I am in Christ" declarations in your daily
   prayer time by praying them out loud until your heart and mind
   embrace the truth of who you are as a new creation in Jesus.

CHAPTER SEVEN

Healing the Pain

⁵…And by His stripes we are healed (Isaiah 53:5).

¹³[F]orgiving one another, if anyone has a complaint against another; even as Christ forgave you, so you also must do (Colossians 3:13).

When you respond to God's grace and His call on your life to be free from pornography, you are going to have to face pain to a degree, probably, that you have never experienced before. I've heard it said many times, by many people, "Pain seeks pleasure." This is a true statement. We are wired as human beings to try and avoid pain. Whenever we hurt our physical bodies, we do whatever is in our power to escape pain, whether it's taking medication or seeing a physician or a chiropractor. The same is true of our heart and soul. When you have given yourself over to sexual sin and a pornography addiction has developed, it exists because there is pain in your heart.

You may not yet be consciously aware of the pain in your heart that is leading you into this addictive behavior. I know that when Jesus freed me from pornography's grip I really started to face the pain in my life for the first time. Sometimes I spent 2 or 3 hours just crying. At first I didn't know what was happening, but God started to show me areas of my life where I needed to receive His healing.

Because I was short and thin growing up (although I grew taller after high school), I grew up with a sense of powerlessness. I remember once when I volunteered to be in the Seattle Christmas parade and was still very thin. My assignment was to be a toy soldier, which involved my being harnessed into an apparatus that was about twice as tall as I was. The legs were attached to my ankles, the arms were controlled by poles that I held, and this flat, wide toy soldier's body towered over my head. On this most unfortunate day the wind was blowing so strong that when I turned certain corners on the parade route, the skyscrapers no longer offered me protection. In fact, on certain streets it was like entering a wind tunnel. They may as well have strapped a giant kite to me that day! My friend Drew, who was wearing the same costume, and people from the crowd literally had to come off the sidewalk and hold on to me so I didn't get knocked over or swept away by these wind gusts. It's funny looking back on it now, but I sure was glad that somehow I made it to the end of the parade route and that the day was over!

I hated myself for being small and skinny. I always wanted to be strong. I let different events deeply affect me, where I was picked on, looked over, and mistreated by peers and authority figures because I was small. Some of the pain in my heart was there because I had allowed my physical stature to affect the way I saw myself. It became really clear when I was wakeboarding with one of my best friends, Todd, and his son Joshua. I was sitting up on the back of the boat strapping into my wakeboard when all of a sudden Todd pushed me into the water when I wasn't expecting it. I got pretty upset about it and tried to stuff my feelings. Todd jumped in the water because he could tell I was upset even though I wouldn't say anything. I took the last run of the night, and as we pulled the boat out of the water and started to drive home in the SUV, all of my hurt feelings from years of being picked on exploded into tears. Todd was totally caught off guard, but he was very gracious with me. I just began to weep and explained that when he pushed me in the water it brought up all these feelings and memories of being the small guy that everyone would bully just because they could. I was able to identify the pain and the lies that I had lived under that night. That explosion of anger over my inner pain was a gift that enabled me to start embracing God's healing. Todd was there for me and helped me work through some of that hurt.

My stories are kind of funny and, to be honest, pretty light. Many other people have grown up with much more traumatizing pain than I have experienced. Some of you reading this have been abused verbally, emotionally, spiritually, physically or sexually…or even some combination of these. Divorce and the destruction of families have become all too common. Many people are hurting just from things that have happened in their homes. If there are areas of your life that are full of unresolved pain, you need to receive God's healing. We are going to look at the different areas of pain in your life and see how forgiveness and the love of God can bring healing to your heart and soul.

VERBAL AND EMOTIONAL ABUSE

Almost everyone has experienced verbal and/or emotional abuse. These are not exactly the same but they often go together. Whether from parents, coaches, teachers, bosses, friends or family, who among us hasn't borne the brunt of someone else's anger and judgment? As a youth pastor I regularly saw young people dealing with the effects of verbal and emotional abuse. Some young people are bullied almost everywhere they go. I have seen youth that are insulted and put down at home, at school and at church. They feel that they can never escape being on the receiving end of other people's negativity and hateful speech.

We have a tendency to compare our pain in life to that of other people. We trivialize things like verbal abuse and try and tell ourselves that it was "just some words." Oftentimes we tend to live in denial of the pain in our hearts. We will say things like, "Oh well, people are just jerks. I don't care what people think. They were just words; it's not that big of a deal." The Bible takes very seriously the matter of the words we speak. Proverbs 18:21 states, "Death and life are in the power of the tongue, And those who love it will eat its fruit." James 3:8-9 elaborates on this idea: "But no man can tame the tongue. It is an unruly evil, full of deadly poison. With it we bless our God and Father, and with it we curse men, who have been made in the similitude of God." Words have the power of life and death and blessing and cursing. We can be in a world of hurt just by words that people have spoken over us.

Verbal and emotional abuse cause hurt in us that will drive us to addictive behavior if we allow them to go unchecked. Often things that happen in our childhood shape us for the rest of our lives. Satan is after children and youth. Whether it's when children suffer through their parents' divorce, where they often believe that the divorce is somehow their fault (even if the parents say it is not), or whether it's when people repeatedly label someone as loser, pervert, idiot, stupid, etc.; they often end up living out what they are told. People even put t-shirts on their kids that say things like, "Here comes trouble." Such labeling as this is a form of cursing. These and similar beliefs, words and phrases have power to direct people's lives.

Sometimes the effects of verbal and emotional abuse are in the things are not said. This type of abuse comes from neglect. I have met several people through the years who have told me that they never heard their dad say, "I love you." Even more numerous are those who either have barely known or never known their dad. Sometimes children have been left and abandoned. Other times children just were never really talked to and left to figure out life on their own. This may not feel like abuse to some, but it has a damaging effect on its sufferers nonetheless.

MATT'S STORY

Matt had just experienced his second divorce and was absolutely crushed. He suspected that something from his childhood was affecting him but he wasn't quite sure what it was. One day he was sitting with his mother and wanted to talk to her about her relationship with him and his grandpa. Matt's mom hated her father, Matt's grandpa. He drank excessively and was a womanizer. A tyrant at home, he treated his kids more like slaves than children and wouldn't allow them to go to school, but just work in his restaurant. As Matt's mom recounted this story with Matt she mentioned about half a dozen times how much she HATED her dad.

Then all of a sudden Matt's mom switched the conversation and said that she needed to confess something to Matt as well. She look right at him and said, "I HATED you, too, Matt!" It was the same hatred that she had in her voice when describing his grandpa. Matt was shocked. She went on to explain that when she got pregnant, things were very bad between her and Matt's dad. She became very angry about the pregnancy and hated her life at the time. Even before he was born, Matt became the focus of all her anger. After he was born, she rejected and neglected him. Later, when she became pregnant with Matt's younger brother, she took that out on Matt as well.

When Matt was around two years old he came down with a cold. At first his mom neglected him, but when the cold turned into pneumonia, Matt was hospitalized. In 1952, this could have been deadly for a child. The doctors even told Matt's dad that Matt was about to die, or at least end up deaf the rest of his life (neither of which happened). But at this point his mom felt so guilty about the way she had treated her young boy that she vowed to be a good mother. Now, decades later, she asked Matt to forgive her, and he did.

Matt still had a lot of anger he had not dealt with, but a lot of the things he had gone through in his life started to make sense. Throughout his life he had looked for approval through many sexual relationships. He was part of the hippie movement and later, part of the Jesus People movement. Although Matt trusted in Jesus Christ when he was 18, he didn't deal much with the pain in his life at that point. Instead, he abused some drugs and continued to charm countless women into having sex with him. He excelled in his career and performed at the top of his field. His unresolved pain caused him often to be angry with coworkers and demand perfection from everyone. This same attitude resulted in two broken marriages. Pornography use turned him into a full-blown sex addict who was in and out of church throughout his adult life. Everything he had done in life was an attempt to medicate the pain of his heart and the rejection he had experienced as a child.

In 2011 Matt came to realize that there was one major lie he had believed that was destroying his joy and freedom in Jesus: "There is something wrong with you and you can't fix it to make people love you." At the time, Matt was lying on the floor and crying to Jesus, asking and begging Him to end this hell in his life. God spoke to Him that day and said, "You've never asked Me to heal the terrible wound in your heart from your mother." His conversation with his mom was back in 1994. He knew that had affected him all those years, but he had assumed that knowing about it meant that it was over. Now, on this day in 2011, he realized that was not the case. He felt the devil still had access to use this pain in his heart against him. Matt asked Jesus to heal him that day and the truth went from his head to his heart in an instant. Healing started that day. Through a process of loving his Lord Jesus, Matt was able to have his mind and thoughts renewed. The bondage to performance in business and sexual sin was broken. God's love had healed his broken heart.

Words and actions that lead us to believe that we are stupid, worthless or inferior in any way are abusive. We need to acknowledge the pain that is happening in our hearts. The point is not to dwell on the pain or live in the pain, but to acknowledge the pain, to be honest about how it has hurt us and to call it what it is, so that we can invite God in to heal it.

Spiritual Abuse

Spiritual abuse is not something that everyone has experienced, but it is common enough to bring up. I personally have not had to deal with this, but I have had friends who were hurt emotionally and verbally by church leaders. When church leaders become self-serving and use their position of authority to hurt others, they inflict not only verbal and emotional abuse on their victims, but often spiritual abuse as well. The result for the victims is a diminished (or destroyed) desire to know God or be a part of the church. This is because the hurtful church leaders represent Jesus (supposedly).

The church is supposed to be a place that protects people who are hurting. Through the prophet Ezekiel, God warns the leaders of Israel because they were called to be as shepherds that protected the sheep but instead were using the sheep for their own selfish gain:

> *⁴The weak you have not strengthened, nor have you healed those who were sick, nor bound up the broken, nor brought back what was driven away, nor sought what was lost; but with force and cruelty you have ruled them. ⁵ So they were scattered because there was no shepherd; and they became food for all the beasts of the field when they were scattered. ⁶ My sheep wandered through all the mountains, and on every high hill; yes, My flock was scattered over the whole face of the earth, and no one was seeking or searching for them* (Ezekiel 34:4-6).

Some of my friends have been in situations where the church sided with a predator rather than the victim in a situation involving sexual solicitation. Other friends have lived through experiences where their pastor told them that if they ever left his ministry their lives would be cursed and they would never have a good spiritual life outside of their church. Another friend opened up about their personal sin only to have people in the church tell lies about them instead of helping to restore them. A pastor friend of mine had a girl from another church come in for prayer because at her church the youth pastor had been having a sexual relationship with her. All of these situations are examples of spiritual abuse (among others).

Godly leaders in the church should not be hurting people. They should be humbly helping people who are hurting and protecting those who are weak. If you have been through experiences like this or in a different way, where pastors or church leaders have threatened you for leaving or have exploited you in any way, you have experienced spiritual abuse. God wants you to know that He is not like that and does not endorse leaders like that. He loves you and wants you to know that although some of His followers have misrepresented Him, He can heal you and cause you to trust Him and be a part of the church again.

PHYSICAL ABUSE

Physical abuse is when someone intends to harm your physical body in any way, shape or form.[16] This may involve being hit, punched, kicked, pushed, bitten or cut. Any way that you are being harmed physically in your body by another, that is physical abuse. Physical abuse not only hurts the body; it hurts the heart and soul. People who are bullied or repeatedly harmed physically have a lot to deal with emotionally. Fear and anger are two things that result from this kind of treatment. No one deserves for their person to be violated. It is not right for people to force their body on yours in any way. Jesus tells us in Matthew 19:19, "You shall love your neighbor as yourself." Jesus condemns violence and physical abuse; it is a violation of love for one's neighbor.

LARRY'S STORY

One man I know, whom we will call Larry (not his real name), said that when he was young he was beaten up on a regular basis. He developed a severe anger problem, and in his teens became very strong. Out of his anger, he became a real brawler and started regularly beating people. One day, he was so out of control that he even beat up his own dad. He finally realized he had to heal up inside and deal with the pent-up anger resulting from all those people hurting him in his early years.

Larry grew up asking, "What's wrong with me? Why am I getting beaten up on the way home from school? Why is my dad smacking me around? WHAT IS WRONG WITH ME?!" On the back of his 8th grade picture Larry wrote: "This is a picture of a nobody." Larry characterized his early life as dominated by feelings of worthlessness.

Fantasy, masturbation and pornography started for Larry around this time in the 8th grade. His mom died suddenly and his dad increased his alcohol consumption to the numb the pain of losing his wife. Larry's dad would come home drunk and beat up Larry and his sisters. Larry remembers that when his mom died, he felt homesick like a little kid spending the night for the first time at a friend's house and just wanting to go back home. But he felt homesick in his own home. He just wanted things to return to normal. He wanted his mom back and he wanted his family back.

Anger and rage started to consume Larry so much that one day he kicked his dad in the groin and his dad started throwing up blood. Larry's sisters gathered around their dad and carried him into the house like an injured football player being carried off the field. While they were carrying him, Larry started circling around them yelling and cursing at his dad. For one of the first times Larry felt a sense of justice and a certain amount of control that gave a foothold for violence to stand its ground. Larry started to realize that violence gave him control and power, which gave him a sense of security as well.

Larry picked up an identity of acting insane, like biting a piece of glass or doing other crazy things. The abused had become the abuser. He picked fights and beat many people up. He thrived on intimidating people. Throughout high school Larry was addicted to pornography, which he sought to give himself comfort from his inner pain. Masturbation had control over him, driving him to indulge multiple times a day. He even turned to using drugs to cope with his pain.

At age 18 Larry had an encounter with God. He had hit a low in his life and used cocaine to get as high as he could. He realized that he was overdosing and needed the OD clinic. When he called for his sisters to help him, he discovered that his voice was non-existent. His pulse was down to once every 6 seconds. It suddenly dawned on Larry that he was about to die. At that moment God spoke to him and said, "Larry, you are dying, but if you come My way you will have peace on this earth and eternal life." Instantly, Larry felt relief. The homesick feeling left his heart. Larry knew that God was real and that He loved him and really cared for him.

As time went on, God softened and broke Larry's heart for his dad. Later, Larry and his sisters were able to do an intervention with their dad with an intervention counselor. His dad's response was, "I would have quit drinking a long time ago if I had known that you loved me as much as you do." The love of God healed Larry's heart and the expression of God's love through Larry was able to bring healing to his dad's heart. Eventually, Larry was able to lead his dad and his sisters to faith in Christ because they had seen such a change in him. It was when Larry shared the grace of God with his dad that his dad surrendered His life to Jesus.

Because Larry was able to receive Christ and get healing in his heart, he is no longer controlled by that anger. He continues to go to Jesus when anger at times still tries to gain a place in his heart. He's in the process of growing in Christ's love as pressure comes from the trials of life. Today Larry is a great dad and husband and an inspiring example of those who forgive people who have hurt them. Likewise, God can help you forgive people who have hurt you so that you are no longer controlled by negative emotions.

SEXUAL ABUSE

"[S]exual assault is any type of sexual behavior or contact where consent is not freely given or obtained and is accomplished through force, intimidation, violence, coercion, manipulation, threat, deception, or abuse of authority."[17]

Sexual abuse is a tragic robbing of someone's purity. Studies predict that 1 in 4 women and 1 in 6 men are sexually assaulted in their lifetime. It is possible that these numbers are low considering that sexual abuse is usually underreported by those who have been victimized.[18]

As a pastor it is difficult to hear stories about how people have been damaged by sexual abuse. Sexual abuse is absolutely condemned by God. In 1 Thessalonians 4:3-6, Paul writes, "For this is the will of God, your sanctification: that you should abstain from sexual immorality…that no one should take advantage of and defraud his brother in this matter, because the Lord is the avenger of all such, as we also forewarned you and testified." God will actually avenge those who have been victimized by sexual sin. No one gets away with any sin, whether in this life or the life to come. Anyone who has hurt you sexually will stand before God and give an account for what they have done.

GARY'S STORY

Gary grew up in a home with a mom who was a committed Christian and a dad who rarely went to church. When Gary was 5 or 6 years old, a relative who occasionally babysat him seduced him to play sexual games. Gary was told, "Try this and do that." His innocence was robbed and he felt very conflicted. On the one hand, he felt validated, but on the other hand he felt vexed and slimed by this perversion. Gary also had a babysitter around this same time who would take him into the basement and molest him as well. He was told, "Don't tell. Don't tell anyone. You'll get in trouble."

At one stage, Gary finally had a friend whom he could tell about what was going on. However, his friend just told him, "This is normal. Don't be ashamed. This is what guys are supposed to do with girls!" This left Gary feeling even more conflicted and made him think that he needed to bury his secret of being sexually abused. This state of affairs continued off and on for a couple of years or so until Gary finally realized that this was wrong and stood up to the abusers. As God helped open his eyes at a young age to what was going on, he refused to allow it to continue.

Pornography found its way into Gary's life around the same time that the abuse began. He came across some sexual images in a bush with his friends and ended up hiding it between his mattresses. When he got home the next day, his parents were waiting in his room and holding up the pictures that he tried to hide. They let him know this wasn't okay, but he was so young they probably didn't realize how much it affected him.

Pornography continued to be a struggle throughout his teenage years. Gary's parents were separated at the time he went through puberty, so he was not really able to have a talk about sex, pornography, or even normal questions about his developing body. The only "help" he really got was an encouragement to use condoms. So he took the plunge into more and more pornography through magazine stashes at friends' houses, through TV and later, through the Internet.

By the time Gary was 18-19 years old he was battling suicidal thoughts. In this place of emotional desperation he started going to church again. He was visiting multiple churches and people would call him out and speak into His life. Gary came under great conviction. At the age of 20, Gary had an encounter with Christ that changed His life.

About a year later Gary was feeling great about life. While in the shower one Sunday morning he felt God speak and say that there was something he still needed to deal with in his life. At church that morning the speaker challenged the people about dealing with hidden sin; specifically, hidden sins committed against them by others, such as being molested. The preacher was very bold and extended an intense call for people to come forward to one area of the altar if they had been molested. Gary stood there and resisted going up, but started to feel as though there was a fire at his back, causing him to sweat. In the end he went forward, and during that time of prayer God stripped the shame off of his life. When he went home later, he had a talk with his parents, both of whom were horrified to learn that their son had been violated that way and saddened that he had been quiet about it for so long. Being open, however, brought Gary into healing and brought him closer to his parents.

As God dealt with the shame and abuse in Gary's life, He was also taking away Gary's desire to use pornography. God helped Gary get free from pornography through relationship. It was relationship with others as he prayed with people who affirmed his identity in Christ when he struggled. It was also relationship with God through the Word and God speaking to his heart that brought healing to Gary's heart.

When Gary was mad at God or disappointed in life, he found himself being tugged into pornography. But as God healed the pain in His heart and restored His identity as a son of God, pornography lost its place in Gary's heart.

It is Not Your Fault

Oftentimes I hear of people who have been hurt through sexual abuse believing that something is wrong with them and even that somehow they themselves are to blame for the abuse. Such a personal violation causes people to hate themselves and brings about a lot of confusion. You must know that if you have been abused in any way, it is not your fault. Jesus not only died to forgive you of your sin but also to bring healing to you for the sin that has been committed against you.

Through the cross of Jesus and the work of the Holy Spirit, God's love can bring healing to your heart and mind if you have experienced any kind of sexual abuse. Jesus took stripes on His back before He went to the cross, and the Bible's promise to you is that "by His stripes, we are healed (Isaiah 53:5)." Jesus took all your pain on the cross, and if you open your heart to Him, He can bring healing to your soul.

God's Healing Love

The love of God is the most powerful force in the world. God *is* love (1 John 4:16). God's love for us is completely unconditional. When you open your heart to God you are opening your heart to love. I don't fully understand why people go through all the abuse that they do. I do know that when Adam and Eve partnered with Satan in the Garden of Eden and ate the forbidden fruit, sin entered the world. Along with sin came all the abuse, violence and pain that humanity has experienced through the ages and still suffers from today. You may have a hard time trusting God if you have suffered from any type of abuse, but if you will look to Him in spite of your pain, you will see that God entered the world by taking on human flesh as Jesus. Jesus was fully God and fully man. He came to take on the feeling of what it means to be human. He was beaten and abused and He suffered so He could know what it is like to go through pain just as His creation has.

He did this not only to identify with your hurt and pain but also in order that you could be healed. Jesus was sinless and therefore knows what it is like to be abused when it is not His fault. He was able to declare to His abusers at the height of His pain on the cross, "Father, forgive them, for they do not know what they do" (Luke 23:34). Through Jesus' ability to forgive His enemies, you can receive power to forgive yours. He sealed God's love for us at the cross. When you surrender to Jesus you are surrendering to His love. His love will work as a force in your life to overcome any obstacles that you face.

If you are holding anger towards God, tell Him about it. Open up about your feelings. He is not uncomfortable hearing about the way you feel. You can be totally honest with Him. You will need to release your anger towards Him and ask Him to replace that anger with His love.

HEALING FROM FEAR, REJECTION AND ANGER

God's love is not only able to heal us from our anger but also from our fear. If we have been put down, beaten down or abused in any way, fear becomes a normal part of the way we live. I used to live in great fear on a daily basis. I was afraid I wasn't acceptable to God and always afraid of what others thought about me. Love is the antidote to fear:

> *[17] Love has been perfected among us in this: that we may have boldness in the day of judgment; because as He is, so are we in this world. [18] There is no fear in love; but perfect love casts out fear, because fear involves torment. But he who fears has not been made perfect in love. [19] We love Him because He first loved us* (1 John 4:17-19).

Fear involves torment. Do you understand what that means? Any thoughts that torment you in fear ARE NOT FROM GOD!

When I had all this fear, I would go to my dad and share these thoughts that seemed so real to me. My dad would always look at me and say, "These thoughts are not from your Father in Heaven, John."

I would argue with him. "How do you know? They feel so real!"

He would reply, "These thoughts you are sharing don't have the fingerprints of my Father on them. Your feelings are real, but they are not always right."

I was driven by my thoughts and emotions, but my dad had come to a place where he was driven by God's Word. When you have feelings and thoughts that cause you to want to drift from God, it is because you are not seeing God clearly for the loving God that He truly is. He is a different kind of Father from our earthly fathers. He is a safe place and a shelter from the pain and storms of life.

Satan and the world have given God the Father a bad rap. He is not angry. He is not against you. He loves you and He is for you. He has a remedy for your feelings of rejection. Abuse in any form can cause one to feel shameful and therefore rejected. Shame tells you that you are worthless. Shame attaches itself to your value and self-worth. Shame lies to you that because bad things have happened to you that you are now deeply flawed. Shame tells you that since unloving things have happened to you, you are now unlovable. All these things are lies.

God is a loving Father who will always draw you near to Him. His voice will never push you away. Any voice that pushes you away from God is never God's voice. Part of your healing comes from surrounding the lies that you have believed about God with the truth until the lies are overwhelmed and can no longer remain.

Knowing the love of God brings healing to anger, fear, rejection and shame. Again, this is all because of what Jesus endured on the cross. His rejection means your acceptance. He was shamed by being tortured and hung on a cross so that you could know that you have value and worth before God. Surrender to God's healing love and let

His love flow through you. The love of God brings you into wholeness more than any other thing. God gave us the promise of His fullness through Paul's words to the Ephesians:

> *[17] that Christ may dwell in your hearts through faith; that you, being rooted and grounded in love, [18] may be able to comprehend with all the saints what is the width and length and depth and height—[19] to know the love of Christ which passes knowledge; that you may be filled with all the fullness of God* (Ephesians 3:17-19).

God wants you to know His love in an experiential way, to "know the love of Christ which passes knowledge." How do you know something past knowing it? You experience it. God's love isn't something to only memorize; it is something that needs to flood your heart. The greatest way to let God's love flow in your life is to receive His forgiveness and to forgive others.

Shame and rejection will cause you to hate yourself. If you have been abused in ANY way, it is NOT your fault at all. Your first step is to receive God's love and cleansing and realize that it is not your fault. You can receive encouragement in God's love through the Scriptures, through prayer, worship and through other believers that will walk with you (a group, a pastor, godly friends or a counselor). Don't underestimate the power of community in receiving God's healing love. God's promises became so real to me mainly through others praying the Bible over me and helping me see myself in light of what God says. Reading the Bible and praying alone are great but having conversations and prayer with believers that will strengthen you is an important part of knowing God's healing love.

FORGIVE YOURSELF AND OTHERS

If you have acted out sexually and sinned against God or others, you need forgiveness, as we discussed in chapters 4 and 5. But here I want to remind you to forgive yourself. Oftentimes people will come to a place where they know that God forgives them but they will not forgive themselves. They hold onto their shame in order to punish themselves. If God has forgiven you for your sin as you believe in what He did on the cross in your place, and you confess your sin, stop confessing the same sin over and over and over. It does not help you or anyone else for you to beat yourself up all the time. God already forgave you, so forgive yourself now. Receive His forgiveness. It is time for you to believe God's promises and move forward in God's love.

Forgiving others for the abuse that they have caused you can be difficult. When someone has violated you, it is an injustice. It is totally wrong. And you need to know that just because you forgive someone, it doesn't mean that what they did to you is okay. The actions that others have done against you to abuse you are *always* wrong. As I stated earlier, anyone who abuses you has to stand before God one day, and that person will NOT get away with anything.

Unforgiveness blocks the flow of God's love in our life more than anything else. In Matthew 6:14-15, Jesus said, "For if you forgive men their trespasses, your heavenly Father will also forgive you. But if you do not forgive men their trespasses, neither will your Father forgive your trespasses." Did you catch that? If we don't forgive others, God doesn't forgive us.

You might rightly argue that people who have hurt or disappointed you don't deserve forgiveness. You are right; no one deserves forgiveness for the things they have done. I know I don't deserve forgiveness for my sin, nor does anyone else, but God has offered us forgiveness through Jesus Christ.

You might be asking, "Well, where do I get the strength to actually do this forgiveness thing?" Ephesians 4:32 says, "And be kind to one another, tenderhearted, forgiving one another, even as God in Christ forgave you." As God forgave you in Christ, now Christ Jesus can supply you with the strength you need to forgive others. If you are a believer, Christ lives in you and you can do whatever Jesus empowers you to do. He is with you to help you forgive.

Forgiveness does not mean that the abuse you suffered is okay now. Forgiveness does not mean that you will forget what happened to you. Forgiveness does not mean that your feelings will change right away. Forgiveness is choosing to resist bitterness and letting God be the judge of the other person instead of you. Forgiveness is a choice of obedience. If you keep standing on your choice to obey God's Word on forgiveness, your feelings will eventually line up with your obedience.

Forgiveness is a must for you to be healed of the pain in your heart. You CANNOT heal all the way if you remain unforgiving. But God is very gracious to help you. Forgiveness is one of the greatest miracles in the Bible. You can be a part of that miracle today as you choose to forgive people who have hurt you. Bitterness and unforgiveness only lock you up inside. Free yourself today by agreeing with God and forgiving those who have hurt you. This will be one of the best and most powerful choices that you have made.

The reason I spent so long talking about abuse, pain and unforgiveness in a book about pornography is because these things that are not dealt with are things that drive us to addictive sin like pornography. You cannot take the *eXXXit* out of pornography if you keep unresolved pain in your life. As you allow God to heal you up inside and face the pain in your life, you won't need sinful vices to make you feel better. God will be the one who makes you feel better. God will change your desires and you can actually start getting addicted to Jesus.

ACTION STEPS

1. Forgive others. Here is a prayer to assist you. Pray it out loud. Stand on the promises of God's Word about forgiveness even when you don't feel like it. Your feelings will eventually match up to your obedience.

    Father God, I thank you that you have forgiven me of all my sins because of Jesus shedding His blood

for me. Help me by your grace and strength to forgive others that have hurt me. I have been hurt and wounded by _____.
I choose today to forgive them by your grace. I release _____ to you God.
Let anger and bitterness have no place in me. Thank you for helping me to forgive like you do. Help me to bless those who have hurt me, like you bless me when I have not earned your blessing. In Jesus' name, Amen.

Continuing to pray blessing for people who have hurt you will help your heart stay open to God and to others. It will help your heart stay grounded in love.

2. Forgive yourself. Sometimes the only person that we don't want to forgive is ourselves. Pray this prayer out loud if you have not been released yourself from guilt and shame.

> Father God, thank you that you have forgiven me of all my sins because of Jesus shedding His blood for me. Thank you that you are not punishing me because of my sin but you love me and accept me. Thank you that you have made me new and I am no longer under guilt and shame. Because you don't remember my sins against me and you have forgiven me, I choose to forgive myself right now. Thank you for purchasing me with the blood of Jesus. Thank you that you remove all my condemnation and fill me with your love. I receive your love, Father. In Jesus' name, Amen.

3. Receive God's love.

> Father God, thank you for loving me so much that you sent Jesus to identify with my sin and pain

so that I could be healed. Where I have been abused and rejected I invite you in to heal me. I ask with confidence for you to heal my heart and my soul. I receive your love. Fill me with your love that you displayed through the cross by the power of the Holy Spirit. Thank you for this love that you share with me. Let me live in your love daily as your child. In Jesus' name, Amen.

CHAPTER EIGHT

Walking in the Spirit

⁹*But you are not in the flesh but in the Spirit if indeed the Spirit of God dwells in you. Now if anyone does not have the Spirit of Christ, he is not His* (Romans 8:9).

¹⁶*I say then: Walk in the Spirit, and you shall not fulfill the lust of the flesh* (Galatians 5:16).

You have an amazing Helper in your life. His name is the Holy Spirit. You may not know a lot about the Holy Spirit, but you need Him to make the *eXXXit* from porn and continue to live in the ways of Jesus. The Holy Spirit is God. Many people refer to the Holy Spirit as "it." This is not correct because The Holy Spirit is a Person.

He is the third Person of the Trinity. The Bible teaches that God is One God, but also three Persons. The word we use to describe this truth is "Trinity," which is a combination of the prefix "tri-" (three) and "unity," a tri-unity or a unity in three. So again, God is one God who reveals Himself in three distinct Persons: God the Father, God the Son (Jesus Christ) and God the Holy Spirit. First John 5:7 states, "For there are three that bear witness in heaven: the Father, the Word (Jesus is also called the Word elsewhere in Scripture), and the Holy Spirit; and these three are one."

Some people use illustrations to help us relate to the truth of the Trinity. For instance, water can be in three phases, a liquid, a vapor or a solid (ice). But whether it is liquid, vapor or solid, it is still water. A three-leaf clover is one clover but with three distinct leaves. An egg consists of the shell, the white and the yolk; again, three distinct parts, but still one egg. No illustration can fully explain the deep mystery of the Trinity, but these can help us on our way to better understand the nature of the One true God as revealed in the Bible.

I went into this whole truth about the Trinity to make it clear that the Bible teaches that the Holy Spirit is truly God. He is no less God than the Father or the Son. As Jesus told His disciples in John 16:7, "It is to your advantage that I go away; for if I do not go away, the Helper will not come to you; but if I depart, I will send Him to you." Jesus wants you to know that it was good that He left the planet so that the Holy Spirit could help each believer in Jesus.

HOW IS THE HOLY SPIRIT OUR HELPER?

The Holy Spirit is not weird. In the King James Version of the Bible He is called the Holy Ghost. But He is not spooky. He is a person. In the next several verses, Jesus explains how the Holy Spirit would be our Helper:

> *8And when He has come, He will convict the world of sin, and of righteousness, and of judgment: 9of sin, because they do not believe in Me; 10of righteousness, because I go to My Father and you see Me no more; 11of judgment, because the ruler of this world is judged* (John 16:8-11).

The Holy Spirit convicts the world of sin so that they can believe in Jesus Christ. He convicts of righteousness and reminds us of what Jesus has done on our behalf since He left the planet. He also convicts us of judgment to remind us of the judgment that has come upon Satan, "the ruler of this world."

The Greek word that is translated as "Helper," carries with it the implication that the Holy Spirit comes alongside of us to give us aid, comfort and help. God is here to help you. The Holy Spirit is a Comforter. He wants to walk with you every day. The word conviction can seem so negative to people, but His job of "conviction" is to always draw you closer to Jesus and the Father. Whenever you are feeling pushed away from God, that is condemnation, which is *not* the work of the Holy Spirit. When the Holy Spirit brings up an area of sin or unbelief in your life, it is not to beat you down but to help you remove anything that prevents God's best from working in your life. He wants to comfort you and help you grow closer to Jesus. The last thing the Holy Spirit wants to do is make you feel guilty and beaten up so that you don't want to come to God.

Because He is God, the Holy Spirit is not okay with sin or with us living a life of compromise. He can be lied to, grieved, quenched, insulted and blasphemed. But the way He gets us out of sin and compromise is by comforting us, helping us and giving us power to experience all that Jesus has for us.

The Holy Spirit is in the life of every believer. He is the seal on every believer and the guarantee of our inheritance (Ephesians 1:13-14). You can't have your sin forgiven and believe in Jesus without the Holy Spirit being in your life. The Holy Spirit speaks to us and reminds us of the words of Jesus (John 16:12-15), empowers us to put to death our old ways (Romans 8:13), pours God's love into our heart (Romans 5:5), reminds us of our adoption by God the Father (Romans 8:15-16), prays for us (Romans 8:26), empowers us to witness (Acts 1:8), gives us spiritual gifts (1 Corinthians 12 and 14) and helps us cultivate good fruit in our lives (Galatians 5:22-23). I want you to get excited about who the Holy Spirit is for you as a believer!

God promises throughout the Bible that we are never alone and that He will never leave us. This is accomplished by the work of the Holy Spirit. He is your friend and guide every day. He will steer you away from evil and into the things that God has for you. Think how amazing it is to have God's Spirit living inside you as a tour guide, a help, a strength and a force in your way out of pornography and into a life that honors God.

THE FLESH VS. THE SPIRIT

Galatians 5:17-18 says, "The flesh lusts against the Spirit, and the Spirit against the flesh; and these are contrary to one another, so that you do not do the things that you wish. But if you are led by the Spirit, you are not under the law." The Holy Spirit will lead you away from the flesh. When you walk with the Spirit, you don't need to focus on the law or try to do things in your own strength. If you try to say no to the flesh in your own strength you will fail over and over again. We (in our flesh) are the problem, because we can't get ourselves out of our own problems. But as we depend upon the Holy Spirit, He will cause these fruits to grow in our lives: "love, joy, peace, longsuffering, kindness, goodness, faithfulness, gentleness, self-control" (Galatians 5:22-23).

The fruit of the Spirit is something that grows naturally in the lives of believers who have identified that they are crucified with Jesus and have a new life of surrender to the Holy Spirit. The flesh is all about doing works of sin or works of self-righteousness where we try to earn God's favor. But we receive the Holy Spirit, God Himself, as a Gift. We don't earn this Gift. You can't get freed by the Spirit and then continue in your own strength. You need to cultivate a relationship with God by walking every day with the Holy Spirit.

SUPERIOR PLEASURE

It is not wrong to be a pleasure seeker. The flesh tempts us to please ourselves in pride by our accomplishments or by giving into lustful temptation that gives our bodies temporary pleasure. But the Spirit will give us a superior pleasure as we come to know God more. One of my Bible school teachers used to often say, "What we starve, dies, and what we feed, grows." As you feed your relationship with the Holy Spirit, not only will you not fulfill the lusts of the flesh but you will desire your old ways less. At one point in Jesus' life some of

His followers started to leave Him. So He asked His other followers what they were going to do: "Then Jesus said to the twelve, 'Do you also want to go away?' But Simon Peter answered Him, 'Lord, to whom shall we go? You have the words of eternal life'" (John 6:67-68). This is what happens to the one who walks in the Spirit; he has no greater place to go. Sin and the flesh lose their appeal as you cultivate a lifestyle of walking in the Spirit.

The Bible at times relates the Holy Spirit to a river in our life as believers. "'He who believes in Me, as the Scripture has said, out of his heart will flow rivers of living water.' But this He (Jesus) spoke concerning the Spirit, whom those believing in Him would receive" (John 7:38-39)." In Psalm 36:8 David says that God gives us "drink from the river of His pleasures." The Holy Spirit wants to be a force like a river of pleasure in our life. He wants to be a life-giving relationship from whom we can draw strength, refreshing and renewing. As the Holy Spirit flows in your life you gain a greater desire for God. The river of God satisfies your life and makes you want more and more. A relationship with the Holy Spirit can bring you so much pleasure and joy in your heart that your desire for addiction loses its strength in your life.

THE FILLING OF THE HOLY SPIRIT

In the book of Ephesians, Paul tells believers, "And do not be drunk with wine, in which is dissipation; but be filled with the Spirit (5:18)." The tense of Paul's language here implies that we need to be continually being filled with the Spirit. This is not to be a one-time experience for the believer, but an ongoing and daily experience. The Holy Spirit filling us regularly empowers us against the temptations that try to arouse our old life. Just as Paul made a contrast between drunkenness and the filling of the Holy Spirit, we realize we can get filled up by God so we don't need cheap fleshly imitations in our lives, whether drunkenness, pornography or any other vice.

As I stated earlier in this chapter, the Holy Spirit is in the life of every believer as a seal, so you might wonder why we need to be filled over and over. You might think, do we leak? Do we lose the Holy Spirit? No, we don't lose the Holy Spirit, but we need a daily dependence upon Him and experience with Him. In John 20:22, Jesus breathed on His disciples and told them to receive the Holy Spirit. Then in Acts 1, before He ascends to heaven, Jesus tells the same disciples to wait in Jerusalem until they are baptized in the Holy Spirit. In Acts 2, they receive this baptism, this immersion in the Holy Spirit; great power comes into their lives and they begin to speak in other languages. In Acts 4, the same people that receive the Holy Spirit in John 20 and Acts 2 are again said to be "filled with the Holy Spirit" (Acts 4:31). We know they already have the Holy Spirit, but they were having a fresh experience where they were renewed in the Holy Spirit.

We even see in the Book of Acts that when the apostles came to a group of people that believed in Jesus, they would make sure that they were baptized in water in Jesus' name and that they had an experience of being filled with the Holy Spirit. For instance, in Acts 19:2, Paul asked the Christians in Ephesus: "Did you receive the Holy Spirit when you believed?" We often don't even address this in the church anymore. We just have people believe in Jesus, but people also need the filling of the Holy Spirit. From other Scriptures we know that all believers in Jesus have the Holy Spirit, but they need an experience with His filling, or a baptism in Him as Jesus says in Acts 1.

The clearest evidence in the New Testament that someone received the Holy Spirit was the evidence of speaking in tongues, which happens in Acts 19 right after Paul lays hands on these believers (they even prophesied too). The purpose of going into teaching about the Holy Spirit in this book is not to give a discourse on the gift of tongues and the evidence of how we know one is filled. I realize that you may come from a different doctrinal background than I do, and if we disagree on the issue of tongues, I want you to please commit to searching the Scripture and allowing your heart to be open to what the Holy Spirit has for you in your Christian life. The gift of tongues and praying in the Spirit both have been a great help to me in overcoming temptation and living a life free of pornography. If you don't speak in tongues, I have no intention of trying to make you feel like a "second class" Christian. My desire is to simply look to the record of Scripture and invite you to share in what has been an incredible blessing in my life. To overcome sexual sin and temptation we need all the strength and tools in our lives that will help. This is one of those tools, and it is powerful in building you up and helping you overcome depression as you are strengthened in your inner man. One thing that is undeniable according the Scriptures is that we need to experience continual and ongoing fillings of the Holy Spirit.

SPIRIT WALK, SPIRIT TALK

Just as we are invited to walk in the Spirit as believers, we are also invited to talk in the Spirit (or pray in the Spirit). Paul said in 1 Corinthians 14:5 that he wished everyone would speak in tongues. In the same chapter, Paul also says that we are to pray both with our understanding and with our spirit. "Understanding" refers to praying in our native language that we can understand, where "spirit" refers to praying through the Holy Spirit with the gift of tongues, where we speak other languages through our spirit, either heavenly or from another nation (1 Corinthians 13:1, Acts 2).

In Jude 20, we learn that we as believers build ourselves up in our "most holy faith, praying in the Holy Spirit." Praying in tongues in the Holy Spirit is a huge strength to our faith. We build ourselves up in the faith through this awesome gift. However, I must issue a WARNING here: If we have tongues or other gifts but do not demonstrate love or good character, then we are deceiving ourselves into thinking we are truly spiritual. If you speak in tongues and yet continue in pornography, pride or rebellion, you are not really living a Spirit-filled life.

This is not an exhaustive teaching, but is meant to ask you to seek God for all the Holy Spirit has for you. Ask to be filled with the Holy Spirit. Ask to speak in tongues. Ask for God to help you grow in all the gifts the Holy Spirit has for you.

101

As you are filled with the Holy Spirit you will be strengthened daily to overcome temptation and put your old ways behind you. As the Holy Spirit fills you, there will be no places in which to hide sin in your life. The more you are filled with Him the more you will be like Jesus, the more you will love the Bible, and the more you will want to obey what God has for you. The Holy Spirit gives us boldness, gives us spiritual gifts and, more importantly, helps us to become more Christ-like in our character.

ACTION STEPS

1. Thank the Holy Spirit for being involved in your life and ask Him to help you walk in God's ways.

2. Pray to receive or be refilled by the Holy Spirit. You can use the following prayer. It would be even better to pray this with other believers or a pastor who knows about the ministry of the Holy Spirit.

> Holy Spirit, thank you for being in my life. Fill me up freshly today. Jesus, baptize me anew. Give me Your power. Stir up my desire for God. Speak to me. Use me today for your glory. Release your gifts in me. Be in my life like a river. I drink of Your Living Water today. Make me more like Jesus. I receive you right now. Thank you, God, that you promised that if I asked for the Holy Spirit you would give Him to me because you are a good Father who gives good gifts to those who ask (Luke 11:9-13).

3. Wait on the Holy Spirit and believe for a fresh baptism of His power. If you feel some words that He is stirring in your heart that don't make sense to your mind, start to say them out loud and keep saying them. The Holy Spirit is praying through you in other tongues or languages.

4. Thank Him for filling you. Continue to use this gift of tongues in your prayer life.

   Whether you speak in tongues or not, continue daily to pray and ask for the Holy Spirit to help you, fill you and baptize you. The devil often gets believers to doubt their experience with the Holy Spirit or gets them to be afraid that if they ask God for the gift of tongues, the devil might jump in and fill their mouth with a false language. The problem with this thinking is that it makes the devil too big and goes against Scriptures such as Luke 11. God so longs to give you the Holy Spirit; it is easy to receive through simple faith the things that He has for you. Don't be stressed or worried if you don't feel much happen right away (being filled is not about your feelings). Stay confident in God's ability to give to you what you need and keep your heart open to Him. There are certainly false gifts and tongues that the devil uses, but they don't come from surrendering to God and asking Him for gifts. They come from a heart that is against God and in rebellion. If your desire is for Jesus and to honor Him, then you are going to receive by His grace the gifts He has for you. Don't give in to fear, but be open in faith.

CHAPTER NINE

Rewiring the Mind

¹I beseech you therefore, brethren, by the mercies of God, that you present your bodies a living sacrifice, holy, acceptable to God, which is your reasonable service. ²And do not be conformed to this world, but be transformed by the renewing of your mind, that you may prove what is that good and acceptable and perfect will of God (Romans 12:1-2).

²⁰But you have not so learned Christ, ²¹if indeed you have heard Him and have been taught by Him, as the truth is in Jesus: ²²that you put off, concerning your former conduct, the old man which grows corrupt according to the deceitful lusts, ²³and be renewed in the spirit of your mind, ²⁴and that you put on the new man which was created according to God, in true righteousness and holiness (Ephesians 4:20-24).

Giving ourselves over to pornography causes our mind to become corrupt. You will remember from chapter 2 that pornography use actually causes damage to the brain. Thankfully, God prescribed something thousands of years ago that science confirms today: you need to change the way you think. The mind has to do with both physical and spiritual components. Pornography damages the part of your soul called the "mind," but it also damages your physical brain. According to Ted Roberts, in an interview at ICSEX, since 1995 science has confirmed that we can change our brain matter.[19] I will reemphasize some of his points about this later in another chapter as well. So, we need not only our physical brain "rewired" as the result of addiction, but also our minds.

You are not stuck with the way you think! As I stated earlier, God supernaturally intervened in my life and brought me freedom from pornography and masturbation. But I had a deep problem with my mind, and there was a process that I needed to walk out to continue in my freedom. You may *eXXXit* out of pornography quickly, but you need to enter into a new mindset to continue in freedom. Being a follower of Jesus is a journey, as is putting your mind back together after having it damaged for so long. Through the power of God's Word, His Spirit, and loving friendships God helped me change the way I think. I used to believe the lie that I was stuck with the thoughts that I had. I used to be so afraid of never being able to change the way I think. There were certain thoughts from my past that literally tormented me every day. (We will talk more in the next chapter about how Satan attempts to bind us and how we can defeat his influence in our lives). Over time, though, God brought healing to my mind, and I realized that I could go a couple of days without certain thoughts that once plagued me. Then I would go a week or so and suddenly notice that the thoughts that once tripped me up no longer had power over me. Sometimes I still find myself in a moment in God's presence when I just begin to gently weep in thankfulness for how God has changed my mind. "With God all things are possible" (Matthew 19:26). I have faith for you. If you are trapped in a cycle of lust, shame and negative thinking, God is able to help you! Don't lose heart. I am going to share some keys that will help you.

THE POWER OF SCRIPTURE

We need to replace the negative thoughts, not just with positive thoughts but with the truth of God. Jesus stated in John 8:31-32, "If you abide in My word, you are My disciples indeed. And you shall know the truth, and the truth shall make you free." I used to think that truth was facing up to all the bad things I had done. There is certainly an element of our freedom that comes from being honest about our past, but once we face up to the sin in our past we need to become familiar with the truth of God's word and the person of Jesus. I was confused because I gave more power in my thoughts to the "facts" of my past rather than the "truth" that Jesus forgave me and made me new. Jesus taught that the purpose of the Scriptures was to give people an encounter with Him. He warned the Pharisees in John 5:39-40, "You search the Scriptures, for in them you think you have eternal life; and these are they which testify of Me. But you are not willing to come to Me that you may have life." As you use the Scriptures you are encountering living Truth; you are encountering Jesus, and the truth of Him and His words will transform your thinking.

Just memorizing a list of Bible verses will not be sufficient to change the way you think. You must mix the Word of God with faith (Hebrews 4:2). As you memorize and believe the Bible and allow your heart to meet with Jesus through the Scriptures, you can specifically change the way you think.

You will need to renew your thinking in several areas, such as how you see God, how you see yourself, how you see the world around you and how you view sex. Don't worry; it might seem like a lot, but if you are walking with God in this process, you can trust Him to do His work and help you renew your thinking. There are a few areas that I would like to touch on when it comes to changing your thinking.

1. *How you see God.* God is good. He loves you. He is holy but not in a way that makes you unworthy to approach him. Many people have not seen God as a loving Father who is *for* them. If you feel like God is against you, you need to see Him for who

He truly is. Oftentimes people like Jesus but have a tough time seeing God as a good Father. Well, Jesus said in John 14 that if we have seen Him (Jesus) then we have seen the Father. If you like Jesus, then trust me, you like the Father also. They are One. God loves you more than anyone else ever could and only has your best interest in mind. Challenge your beliefs and thoughts if they don't line up with this reality.

2. *How you see yourself.* It is easy to see the negative but you must know how valuable you are to God. You have to discover your worth to walk in freedom. My friend Todd White often teaches that if you feel depressed, discouraged, hopeless, condemned and the like, you have no future. Remember that is what the devil feels like. He is depressed, discouraged, hopeless, condemned and has no future. He is trying to reproduce his identity and mindset in you. That is why it is so important to spend time learning about and confessing who you are in Christ (see the end of chapter 6).

3. *Sex.* Sex is not gross, porn is. Sex is a gift from God for creating children and enjoying pleasure between a husband and wife in marriage. When you use sex wrongfully outside of marriage between a man and woman or through pornographic behavior, you start to regard sex as something that is dirty and shameful. As people get married who have been addicted to pornography, they often find it difficult to retrain their mind to realize that sex in marriage is not only okay, but is actually a beautiful thing in which God is glorified.

4. *Seeing others as people and not objects.* This can happen both with men and women, but tends to happen to men more often because God made men to be so visual. Pornography programs men to see women as an object to be used for their own lustful pleasures. Paul instructed Timothy to treat "older women as mothers, younger women as sisters, with all purity (1 Timothy

5:2)." Men, we are called to build healthy relationships with women in purity. We have to start changing our thinking about how we look at women so that we won't degrade them as objects to be used. This is a far cry from what our culture paints as a picture of relationships between men and older and younger women. There is a Biblical principle that I have heard various people share: "What the law demands, grace provides." In other words, if God tells you to do something in the Bible, such as treat women a certain way, His grace will empower you to live that out as you desire to obey Him. Satan has a great hatred for women, and this hatred is a primary fuel behind the power of pornography. We need to have our hearts and minds turn away from the hateful use of women (and men as well) and have a love and tenderness for people the way God does.

5. *Thinking about good things.* Colossians 3:2 says, "Set your mind on things above, not on things on the earth." Some people say, "Don't be so heavenly minded that you are no earthly good." This is correct in the fact that you don't need to act super spiritual all the time and not be able connect with others in a meaningful way. But if we think about what God thinks about more often, we will have our minds saturated with healthy thoughts. As I shared earlier, what you starve, dies, and what you feed, grows. You need to starve these earthly thoughts and feed thoughts about God and His beauty, majesty, love and forgiveness. As you focus on and fill your mind with thoughts that are rooted in heaven, the pressures of earth become less and less of a force to dominate you. Even when you go through hard things, when your mind is set on the right things you can face trials in a way that honors God.

TOOLS FOR USING THE BIBLE TO RENEW YOUR MIND

1. Take a piece of paper and make a list with two columns. In the first column, make a list of lies that you have believed about yourself,

sin or struggles that you have been going through. In the other column begin to write out a list of God's truth that counters that situation you are going through. For example, in the left column, if you are struggling with receiving forgiveness, you should write down the lie, "I am unforgivable" or "God won't forgive me." In the right column use a Bible verse like Colossians 1:14, "in whom we have redemption through His blood, the forgiveness of sins." Complete a list of lies and God's truth. Then start using this list daily in your prayer time. Confess God's truth over your life, out loud every day.

2. Pray Romans 6. My dad gave me this tool and it is one of the most beneficial things I did to renew my thinking. I would read and memorize Romans 6, and every place that the word "sin" appeared I would replace it with a specific sin, such as "lust" or "pornography," thus personalizing the chapter. My reading and declaration of Romans 6 would go something like this:

> What shall John Hammer say then? Shall John Hammer continue in lust that grace may abound? Certainly not! How shall John Hammer, who died to lust, live any longer in it? Or do you not know, John Hammer, that as you were baptized into Christ Jesus, you were baptized into His death? Therefore, John Hammer was buried with Him through baptism into death, that just as Christ was raised from the dead by the glory of God the Father, even so John Hammer should walk in newness of life. For if John Hammer has been united together in the likeness of His death, certainly John Hammer also shall be in the likeness of His resurrection, knowing this, that John Hammer's old man was crucified with Him, that the body of lust might be done away with, that John Hammer should no longer be a slave of lust."

I would continue this way through the whole chapter. This exercise would force me to daily confront my heart and mind with the power of the gospel. I was reminded that my freedom really comes through what Jesus has done for me. At first I had great doubts as I did this, but over time I became convinced of God's acceptance of me and that I was a new person because of what Jesus had done for me.

3. Scriptural memorization and meditation. Memorizing Bible verses is important and meditating on the Bible is a powerful way to renew your mind. Biblical meditation is not about emptying your mind, but about filling it with God's Word and meditating on who God is. I used to write key Bible verses onto 3x5 cards and take them to work with me. I needed God to help me through fear and shame a lot. So a lot of my verses were about peace of mind, God's love and the power of the gospel. When I was on a break at work or waiting to meet someone in the day I would pull out some cards from my back pocket and read them over and over to memorize them. But I would also focus on each word and try to extract every ounce of power in each word. It's like when you are finishing your favorite bowl of ice cream and you keep scraping the bowl to make sure that you get every last drop. Meditation is when you try and get every last drop of truth out of each Scripture you are using.

4. Guarding your influences. If you give your mind a lot of inputs that are perverse, depressing and dark, you will end up thinking about things that are perverse, depressing and dark. When God freed me from pornography, I started to quickly notice that a lot of media I consumed was fueling my depression and tempting thoughts. Without anyone giving me a list or telling me what I should or shouldn't do, I started getting rid of a lot of my music. My music was mostly about sad and depressing things like loneliness and broken relationships. It fueled my negative emotions. Then I noticed that a lot of movies and television programs I

watched, although not considered pornography, had so many sexual references that, because of my past, fueled impure thoughts in my mind. I had to cut off certain programs and movies. We will cover this a little bit more in chapter 11.

5. Prayer and Presence. There is something powerful about cultivating a friendship with God and spending time with Him. You need to get alone in His presence (I recommend every day!). Spend time in the presence of God, silently waiting on Him, where you pour out worship to Him and talk to Him out loud about what you are going through. Spend time also listening to His voice. When I spend time with people, they have an influence on me and the way I think. As you spend time talking, listening and waiting on God, you will start to think more like He does.

6. A group project. We experience a lot of change in our thinking through loving friendships and community. You can't dig yourself out of this mess by yourself. We will also cover this more in chapter 11.

CHAPTER TEN

Shattering Strongholds

³For though we walk in the flesh, we do not war according to the flesh. ⁴For the weapons of our warfare are not carnal but mighty in God for pulling down strongholds, ⁵casting down arguments and every high thing that exalts itself against the knowledge of God, bringing every thought into captivity to the obedience of Christ, ⁶and being ready to punish all disobedience when your obedience is fulfilled (2 Corinthians 10:3-6).

¹⁰Finally, my brethren, be strong in the Lord and in the power of His might. ¹¹Put on the whole armor of God, that you may be able to stand against the wiles of the devil. ¹²For we do not wrestle against flesh and blood, but against principalities, against powers, against the rulers of the darkness of this age, against spiritual hosts of wickedness in the heavenly places (Ephesians 6:10-12).

You are in a war for your purity! A battle is raging for your soul. You may not have realized it, but your battle to get free from pornography is more than just something that is going on inside of you. The devil is out to destroy your life and he will do everything he can to prevent you from making the *eXXXit* out of a lifestyle of sin. The Bible refers to this unseen enemy of God and man as the devil, Satan, Lucifer, the father of lies and the list could go on. In the Book of Revelation, Satan is described as a deceiver and an accuser (Rev. 12:9-10). He tempts, pressures and bullies people to compromise their purity and afflict trouble on the world around them. The three areas he uses to work against you are your flesh, the world's system and the demonic realm.

The Flesh

The devil loves to remind Christians of their past and put their old identity on them. He does this by accusing us that God won't forgive us or accept us; that we are still bound to our old sin that has already been paid for by the cross of Jesus Christ. The Bible declares, "Those who are Christ's have crucified the flesh with its passions and desires" (Galatians 5:24). As we learned earlier in chapter 6, we need to identify with the death, burial and resurrection of Jesus. If we don't count ourselves dead to sin and live in the power of God's grace, we will almost certainly compromise in our flesh. After we become Christians, it is still possible to sin. If we don't manage our desires by the help of the Holy Spirit, we can operate out of our flesh that has already died with Jesus. Don't dig up your flesh and give it life again. The devil will use things in our body, our flesh, to get us to compromise our purity. Remember, it's not a sin to have sexual desire. It's a sin to act out upon that desire outside of God's ways.

The World's System

The devil is behind propagating his influence through the system of the world. First John 2:15-17 states, "Do not love the world or the things in the world. If anyone loves the world, the love of the Father is not in him. For all that is in the world—the lust of the flesh, the lust of the eyes, and the pride of life—is not of the Father but is of the world. And the world is passing away, and the lust of it; but he who does the will of God abides forever."

If we love the world's ways, God's love can't be in us. The world promotes the lust of the flesh, the lust of the eyes and the pride of life. We see this in the media. We see this in what is considered "popular" in a culture. The world tries to press you into its way of life. Many people make choices simply because they feel that "everyone else is doing it." It's interesting to me how as a pastor people will often tell me that they gave in to a certain behavior that is sinful after they discovered that someone they knew personally had tried it or introduced it to them. Doing something because someone else did it is one of the worst reasons to do anything.

The reason I dedicated a whole chapter to renewing the mind is because we must be vigilant to change the way we think to conform to God's ways. As you think like God thinks, your desires will not be for the passing pleasures that this world has to offer. Living in the world's ways will leave you empty and without an identity. The enemy knows this and that's why he tries so hard to make sin appear fun. From the outside a life of immorality might look glamorous, romantic and even powerful. But what you don't see in TV, movies or magazines is all the abuse, addiction, diseases and fear that people live under in the sex industry.

THE DEMONIC REALM

The demonic realm is the realm of fallen angels that Satan rules. Satan was at one time known as Lucifer. He was believed to be a high-ranking angel but decided he wanted to be lifted up above God in pride and become an object of worship (Isaiah 14). God was forced to remove him from heaven. In Revelation 12:4 we also learn that Satan in his rebellion took one third of the angels with him, which are now known as fallen angels, demons or evil spirits. Ever since Satan rebelled against God he has set his sights on destroying the work of God in the earth. Just as God wants to give you an identity from Him, Satan is looking to put his identity upon mankind and bring about as much destruction as he possibly can.

Satan and his demonic assistants are not able to read the mind of man, but for thousands of years they have been studying human behavior. They use thoughts, feelings, experiences, impressions and other people to get us off track. As you read from 2 Corinthians 10 at the beginning of the chapter, the realm of our thoughts, the mind, is where Satan looks to build strongholds in us. If Satan can use thoughts, feelings, experiences, impressions and other people to get us to agree with Him, he can dominate our thinking. The mind truly is the battlefield where this spiritual war takes place.

In my own life this was a major hindrance for me. When you agree with a lie of Satan or give yourself over to a repetitive sin, not only can you develop an addiction in your body but you can also become a slave spiritually through Satan establishing a stronghold in you. A stronghold is a place where Satan has a strong hold or strong influence over you. I discovered after I had originally desired to be free that I had opened a door for the demonic to bring destruction to me and I needed to kick out these intruders.

I want to be careful to let you know that we must not blame the devil for sin that we have chosen to commit. The devil doesn't make us do anything. But the demonic realm can have access to us when we allow them in, and if the demonic is a present force that is influencing our lives, we need to deal with it God's way.

Shortly after I began opening up to my dad about my problem with pornography, I read a book about how the devil gains an influence in our lives. It freaked me out big time! But ultimately it led me to learn the importance of prayer and spiritual warfare so that I could be free from the influence of the devil. My dad had been away on a trip and returned home right after I finished the book. I decided to open up more fully about what I had been dealing with. So we prayed together right then and on a few other occasions where I literally had the devil's hold broken off of my life.

The reason I put this chapter later in the book is because I firmly believe that we must understand the basic message about how the power of Jesus on the cross and His resurrection are the basis for our freedom from pornography. What Jesus has done for us is also the basis of what stops the work of the demonic in our lives. If you kick the demons out of your life but don't believe firmly in God's love for you through the cross, the demons will soon rush back in to harass you even worse. If you kick the demons out of your life but don't decide to build healthy, accountable friendships and continue to grow in God's Word, then their influence can return to where it was before.

A lot of people are afraid of the demonic, but in all actuality, if you have submitted to God and you resist the devil, then James 4:7 clearly says that the devil must "flee from you." You need to understand and believe that when you point your will in the same direction as God's will, all of heaven will back you up. The devil is actually afraid of you when you are in right relationship with Jesus. God wants you to know who you are in Jesus Christ. The devil fears this so much because he knows that you can cause His kingdom great pain.

The devil never fights fair. He will try and tempt you and put you in situations where people say things to you and push things on you as much as he can. But God is faithful. 1 Corinthians 10:13 promises that "No temptation has overtaken you except such as is common to man; but God is faithful, who will not allow you to be tempted beyond what you are able, but with the temptation will also make the way of escape, that you may be able to bear it." The devil attempts to cut off your hope. As soon as you feel hopeless, you can know for certain that you are listening to the wrong voice. Even though God doesn't tempt us, in the midst of every tempta-tion He has a way of escape. With every temptation, a provision for escape accompanies it.

If you have tried to get yourself out of pornography over and over again with no success, it is quite possible that you have developed a stronghold and the demonic has access to influence you in this area. There is more to do than just dealing with the devil, but it's impor-tant that if he has gotten into your life, that you properly deal with

eXXXit

him so that you no longer have him messing with you to this degree. Dealing with the devil is actually the easiest part of walking in purity (because Jesus has already defeated him and rendered him powerless on the cross), but an important step in your freedom nonetheless.

DISMANTLING STRONGHOLDS

God can dismantle strongholds in our lives. Agreement with God and breaking the agreement of the devil is the most powerful foundational tool to break a stronghold of Satan in our lives. As we read above in 2 Corinthians 10, we take "every thought into captivity to the obedience of Christ." The obedience of Jesus brought about the shedding of His blood through death on the cross, which is the foundation for breaking strongholds. Revelation 12:11 says, "They overcome him (Satan) by the blood of the Lamb and by the word of their testimony, and they did not love their lives to the death."

If you have agreed with the power of what Jesus has done for you, you have taken the biggest step on the right path to porn-proofing your life. Next though, if you are bound, you need to break agreement with the power of the enemy. These strongholds can come into our lives through various means.

Continuing in a specific sin like pornography or masturbation over a long period of time can create a stronghold. Also, when someone sins against us and we don't forgive them, a stronghold of anger or bitterness can develop in our lives. The devil doesn't play fair. If he motivates someone to abuse you, he wants to use that situation against you in every way possible to keep you in fear or anger. Forgiving people who hurt you will dismantle strongholds in your life.

Believing lies and agreeing with them will also put you into bondage to the demonic. If you have ever spoken words over yourself like "I'm stupid," "I'm fat," or "I'm ugly," then you are cursing yourself. If others have cursed you and you believe what they say, you give those words power over you. If you have believed that you are doomed to continue down this path forever, your faith in Satan's lies is a stronghold.

118

Satan will also attempt to work through families in similar patterns. Oftentimes you see a pattern of sin in a family line. For instance, you might witness that every generation there is divorce, addiction or immorality. Satan wants you to feel powerless and believe the lie that you will be bound by the same things that have destroyed your family in previous generations.

The truth is that because of Jesus, every sin, curse, and power that stands against you can be overcome because Jesus took the weight of the curse upon Himself in our stead so that we can have freedom. Ephesians 4:27 admonishes us to NOT "give place to the devil." We can break agreement with anything that he has brought into our life and we can evict him as an intruder that we no longer want influencing us.

ACTION STEPS

How to Pray

It is important to pray in order to walk in the freedom that Jesus has offered you. I am going to lay out some sample prayer steps here that you can pray, but praying as a lifestyle is a very important part of walking in freedom. Pray these prayers OUT LOUD, and preferably with a pastor, counselor, parent or accountability group. These prayers need to be prayed with authority and faith in Jesus' name. If you trust in Christ, DO NOT be intimated by the demonic. Rise up in strength in the promises of God as you pray through this list.

Repent

Father God, thank you for the sacrifice of Jesus on the cross for all of my sin. Thank you that Jesus won the victory over sin, the devil and demons for me. I confess that I have sinned against you, God, and opened the door for demonic strongholds in my life. I take responsibility for my choices to sin and I ask you to forgive me and cleanse me for _____ (list whatever you need to: pornography, sexual books, homosexual sex, lesbian sex, lust, masturbation, fantasy, all sexual relationships outside of marriage, orgies, phone sex, cybersex, strip clubs, etc.). Thank you that you forgive me for all my sin, the ones that I remember and the ones that I don't. By your grace I choose to turn away from these things and submit my life to you, God. I yield my heart and spirit to you in Jesus' name.

Renounce

I thank you, Jesus, for how you destroy the power of all demonic influence and strongholds in my life by the power of your obedience to death on a cross. I renounce every place where I have given over to evil spirits in my life. I renounce the power of _____ (list out loud lies you have believed, specific experiences that hurt you, specific sins or emotions, anger, unforgiveness, bitterness, generational sins and patterns in your family, etc.). I declare the power of Jesus' blood totally cuts off the influence of all these things in my life. I renounce all sinful and unhealthy ties and bonds I have had with these people _____ _____ (list names of people that you have been sexually involved with in any way). I choose to forgive _____ for all the pain they have caused me (list all people who have hurt you in any way). Thank you, Jesus, that these things have no power over me any longer.

Rebuke

I thank you, God, that as I submit to you and resist the devil, he must flee from me. I rebuke every evil spirit that has had access to influence my life. The influence of _____ is now cut off in my life by the work of Jesus Christ (ask God to reveal to you what spirits have been at work against you, such as: accusing spirits, deceiving spirits. spirits of anger, lust, pride, immorality, addiction, etc.).

Receive

Father God, I receive your cleansing and forgiveness. I receive a cleansing over my body and my brain where I have sinned and I present my body to you, God, to be used for holy living. I thank you that you openly defeated Satan and the demonic on the cross and that I get to share in your victory. I receive a new mentality of victory over the devil. As I have humbled myself today, I receive your grace to me as an overcomer. I thank you that as I humble myself under your mighty hand, you will exalt me in due time. I receive your unconditional love that is in Christ Jesus for me. I receive all that you have for me. I receive the good gifts that you, Father, have for me. I will no longer receive lies from Satan but will receive the truth of what you say. Thank you that your Word is life-giving to me and that you lift me out of condemnation. For all my shame, I receive double honor. For all my heaviness, I receive a lifestyle of praise. For all my depression, I receive joy and peace. Thank you, Father God.

Refill

I also receive a refilling of the Holy Spirit. Daily, I ask to be filled with fresh power and strength from the Holy Spirit. Holy Spirit, thank you that you pour the love of God into my heart. Thank you, Holy Spirit, that you fill up every place in me. Where old mindsets and sin once filled me, thank you that now you fill me with new mindsets and remind me of the new identity that I have in Jesus Christ. Fill me up to overflowing. Thank you, Jesus, that you promised that rivers of living water would flow from my inner-most being. I am renewed, refilled and refreshed by your work, Holy Spirit.

Replace

Father God, thank you that I can do all things through Jesus Christ who gives me strength. Thank you that you give me power to replace old habits with new healthy ones. Thank you that you replace negative thoughts with God-given positive ones. Thank you that you help me to replace the negative use of my time with a healthy use of time. Thank you that you empower me to have healthy relationships with men and women, instead of negative and selfish ones. Thank you that you help me to overcome temptation in your power and not in my own strength. Father, replace my old desires with new ones. I am dependent on you, God, and the work of the Holy Spirit. With you all things are possible. Thank you for your help, Lord Jesus. Thank you for loving me. In the all-powerful name of Jesus I pray these things, AMEN!

CHAPTER ELEVEN

Flee—Pursue—
Along With

*²²So flee youthful passions (lusts) and pursue righ-
teousness, faith, love, and peace, along with those who call
on the Lord from a pure heart* (2 Timothy 2:22 ESV).

This verse has been a key Scripture for me making the *eXXXit* out
of pornography and into purity. Paul writes to the young leader Timothy and gives him three practical steps for dealing with lust. When
you take any one of these three steps by themselves you will probably
see some positive differences in your life. But when you combine all
three you have a powerful force at work in your life to bring you into
victory over sexual sin.

First, Paul told Timothy to "FLEE youthful lusts." We are often
told within the church to "flee" sin. It might come out as, just say
"no" to sin or say "no" to sex outside of marriage. However, just saying no to something without having a deeper "yes" in your heart to
the right thing usually ends in sabotage. That's because if you only
focus on a negative, you will end up living out that negative because
it is all you think about.

Going further, Paul shares that not only should you flee the
wrong, but now you must also "PURSUE righteousness, faith, love,

and peace." In order to get away from sin we also need to go after godly character qualities that honor God.

Lastly, Paul adds one more part to this recipe for overcoming. It's like he is saying, "It's not enough to say no to sin and yes to right things, Timothy, but you also have to do these things 'ALONG WITH those who call on the Lord from a pure heart.'"

Let's dig deeper into each part of this Scripture and see how we can live this out.

FLEE

Lust is something that we are supposed to flee. That means to run or get away from it just as fast as we can. Sometimes people believe that self-control is putting themselves in a place where they are heavily pressured to sin and just saying no. True self-control is staying away from those places and situations in the first place.

The Bible tells us to resist the devil (James 4:7) and that we wrestle against demonic forces (Ephesians 6:12). But sometimes people get confused. They think that since we resist and wrestle our spiritual enemies, we should struggle with and fight temptation. This is not so. The best way to defeat temptation is not to engage it in battle but simply to run away from it!

One day I went to a local beach. There is a place there where I like to go with my Bible and journal. I sit up on some large rocks by some train tracks and the salt water gently rolls against the rocks several feet below where I sit. I go to pray, hear God and plan about the future.

Well, on this particular visit, a young lady with a couple of photographers came over towards where I was sitting in anticipation of some awesome God time! The next thing I knew, they started to do a bikini photo shoot right next to me, even as I was seeking the face of God. Our beaches in the Puget Sound aren't quite like California, where the whole beach is covered with people in bathing suits on the sand. Our beaches are beautiful but they are full of rocks. This was not a common occurrence at this beach.

I remember feeling frustrated, because I was there first and was doing something "spiritual." But I realized very quickly that I needed to get out of there if I was going to keep my mind pure. I didn't try and fight it on that day; I decided to just get out of there. I fled away from an opportunity to lust that day. There were plenty of times earlier in my life when I would try and reason with myself that it was okay to hang around a compromising situation. Those times always ended with my giving in to sexual temptation.

When we are tempted to lust, we may face another temptation to dig inwardly for the reason why we are being tempted. There certainly is a place for allowing God to examine our heart and bring healing and freedom to places inside of us that are drawing us to desire sin. However, the moment you are being tempted isn't the time to just sit around. What you must do in those moments is get out of there and get out quickly. When temptation comes knocking on your door, RUN, do no walk out of the building!

Lust is a choice. Often people become confused. The devil uses a sexual thought of temptation to cause a believer to feel ashamed and guilty even when they haven't sinned. Lust is a choice, but since it is a choice in the mind that is associated with strong feelings, it is difficult to tell if we are just being tempted in the mind or if we have crossed the line into sin in the mind. James 1:14-15 says, "But each one is tempted when he is drawn away by his own desires and enticed. Then, when desire has conceived, it gives birth to sin; and sin, when it is full-grown brings forth death." It is not a sin to have "desire." If you are a man and see a beautiful woman and have sexual desire stir up in your heart or mind, that is not a sin. It's a temptation. You have not lusted by having a thought. You cross the line into sin, specifically, into lust, when you choose to partner with that desire and make a decision to focus on that thought and let it grow. Like James says here, if your desire conceives, it gives birth to sin and sin gives birth to death. So the time to flee lust is in the desire or temptation phase.

Joseph in the Book of Genesis was at one point given the opportunity to have sex with his boss's wife (Genesis 39). Joseph had a promise from God that He was going to be a great leader one day. His boss's wife approached him on several occasions to sleep with her and was quite persistent. Joseph told her no, but at first he stayed around his job there in the house. Since he had a heart to honor God, when his boss's wife approached him again for sex and grabbed him by his coat, he quickly ran away. He left his coat and his job behind. In fact, even though he did what was right, he was falsely accused. It seemed like nothing was working out for Joseph when he honored God, but God watched out for him. He actually got closer to his destiny as he put God first in everything. Our response to lust needs to be the same as Joseph's. We need to take temptation seriously and FLEE from lust right away, no matter the cost. Don't fight lust, examine lust or toy with lust. RUN AWAY FROM IT!

I have heard Pastor Bill Johnson say, "What you tolerate, dominates." This is a true statement. You cannot be complacent and put yourself in a place where temptation can come easily. Jesus taught His disciples to pray, "Do not lead us into temptation, but deliver us from the evil one" (Matthew 6:13). You must guard your mind and your imagination. Don't beat yourself up when tempted, but don't allow yourself to linger at the place of temptation, either. We must not be deceived about the power of lust and temptation and deal with it quickly when it comes our way. We must have no tolerance for lust in our lives.

Pursue

Pursuing something is the exact opposite of fleeing from it. Fleeing is running away from something, but pursuing is running towards it. As a kid I would do almost anything to get a Slurpee from 7-11. After I woke up in the morning and had cereal and watched reruns of old action shows, it was time to scheme up an idea to get my hands on a Slurpee. There was a size that was 89 cents, and after tax I needed almost one dollar. So I would ask and beg my parents for money to get this Slurpee. When they said no, I would try and mow lawns, collect cans for recycling money, and my personal favorite, dig through couch and chair cushions for spare change. In fact, my dad had one chair that was at the perfect angle for loose change to slide out of his pockets into the cracks under the seat cushions. I would start to dig in the cracks and feel cheerios, cheese crackers and other crumbs. But excitement would flood through me when I could feel a rough edge of a coin and begin to try and pull it out with my fingers working like little tweezers. When I pulled out a quarter, it was like hitting a gold mine. I was almost towards my goal for that Slurpee. That consuming desire to get a Slurpee motivated me to do whatever it was going to take to have my desire fulfilled.

When God has changed your heart by His grace you start to have a desire to honor Him. You need to continue to pursue the things that Paul wrote to Timothy about: "righteousness, faith, love and peace." Most of this book is about the gospel of Jesus, identifying with what Jesus has done for you and changing the way you think. Building your relationship with Jesus is all about pursuing the right things. We can never become satisfied with where we are, but we should always desire to be even more like Jesus. As you starve the thoughts of your past and focus on things of God, your desire to pursue Jesus will grow. It's awesome! The more you have of Jesus, the more of Him you want. Don't ever stop pursuing the things of God. Be on a lifetime journey of possessing more "righteousness, faith, love and peace."

ALONG WITH

I love that Paul didn't stop at just telling young Timothy to stop the bad and go after the good, but also to do this "ALONG WITH those who call on the Lord from a pure heart." One of the biggest keys to living a life of purity has to do with who you spend your time with. Your friends define your future. The founder of the social network Linked In, Reid Hoffman, said, "The fastest way to change yourself is to hang out with people who are already the way you want to be."[20]

Pornography keeps us from healthy relationships. By the same token, healthy relationships will keep us from pornography. Pornography is a shortcut to having our needs fulfilled. Oftentimes we don't realize that some of the needs we are looking for in pornography are not just physical or sexual needs but the need for relationships.

Healthy friendships with others give us a strong feeling of security, fulfillment and joy. Those are things that pornography can only supply in a false and cheap way. You might feel a buzz from pornography for a moment, but it will disappoint you and destroy you after that good, quick feeling. Friendships with people who actually love you and care about your future are a huge key to walk out the *eXXXit*. We are all made to connect in healthy relationships. If you are isolated and don't have close friends that you can really share your heart with, then you are missing out on an important part of your needs being met in a way that God has provided for you.

My youth pastor's mom used to always tell him, "Russ, you're not an island!" What she was instilling in him was the understanding that he couldn't tackle the issues of life alone. She wanted him to know that he needed other people in his life to help him. This is exactly what Paul was trying to get through to Timothy and to us.

When I started to open up with others in my life that I could trust and who really pursued God, I had so much strength against temptation to lust. God brought people into my life who would love me, correct me, challenge me, laugh with me, cry with me and dream with me. It is very important not to underestimate the power of godly friendships. I heard pastor and author Ted Roberts say in an interview about healing from sexual addiction that "we are often wounded in community (with other people) and therefore we usually heal in community."[21]

God is very concerned about the people that we spend time with. In 1 Corinthians 5:9, Paul says: "I wrote to you in my epistle not to keep company with sexually immoral people." He goes on to say that he wasn't implying sexually immoral people who are not Christians, or else how could we let those who are lost know about the hope we have in Jesus? He meant that we are not to spend time with people who say they are Christians but are sexually immoral. This doesn't mean we can't talk to people who are currently struggling with sexual immorality but want to get help and are working on walking in purity. Paul is talking about people who are living in straight up sexual sin and don't think that they need to stop or don't want to stop.

The reason for this is because when someone says they are following Jesus and belong to Him but will continually walk in a certain sin, they are double-minded and deceived. They will affect you negatively. When I was around non-Christians in my life, I wouldn't participate in their sinful discussions; I could clearly see what was right and wrong. But when I was around Christian friends who were openly sinning and talking about things they shouldn't have, I didn't have clear judgment because there was a mixture of what was right and wrong. That is so dangerous because you start to compromise and become like the people you hang out with.

You need to look for acceptance from God first and then also from godly relationships where people have a "pure heart." It is in these friendships where you can practice James 5 together; friendships where you can pray, confess sin and see God bring restoration and forgiveness.

I once heard the leader of Jesus Culture, Banning Liebscher, talk about how when we are in healthy relationships in a church community, we have access to all the best resources of that community. For instance, if you have a money problem and one of your friends is an expert in money, then you can get his advice and help to have breakthrough in your problem. However, if you are isolated and not open with others in your life, then no one knows how to help you and you are left to figure things out by yourself.

Sometimes, when it feels like God isn't answering our prayers, I believe He is telling us no to direct intervention because He has provided help in a friendship that we have or that He wants us to have. I believe this applies to our sexual freedom as well. We want to *eXXXit* porn with three easy steps, do it all by ourselves and move on in life. However, God wants to use this time in our life to learn to trust others and open up with them. I'm not saying that God gave us sin to help us have friendship; I'm saying that He can use our opening up about our sin to develop friendships.

There was a young man whom I was encouraging in a life of purity. He would rarely give in to sexual temptation; about every 6 weeks or so. After I worked with him for a while we began to see a pattern emerge in his life. He would get really overworked, become tired and stressed, and feel lonely. Then he would cave in to temptation and afterwards call me feeling horrible about himself. We prayed, took communion and talked about a lot of things in this book. Our friendship grew stronger. We talked about a plan to overcome this cycle and decided that when this temptation arose again in about six weeks, he would call me *before* he sinned.

One night I was at a special youth event and he knew I was there. When I got out of the youth rally I noticed I had a voicemail from this young man. He told me that he noticed that all those parts of the cycle were in place, and when he identified he was being tempted he called out to me through a voicemail to get strength against this temptation. When we talked a couple of days later, I found out that he didn't cave in to the temptation. He got victory just by leaving me a voicemail. God had given us a friendship and used that friendship as his way to escape temptation. This was a real turning point for this young man to get out of this cycle. Now he is helping other young men *eXXXit* porn in their lives.

Healthy friendships will be such a blessing to you and a place for healing in your life. Start to pursue friendships with people who love God and are going places in their lives where you want to be. Go to small groups or home groups at church. Join an accountability or purity group. Start looking for ways to spend time with people you desire to have friendships with.

ACTION STEPS

1. Are there any places, situations or circumstances from which you need to flee?

2. What is God calling you to pursue at this time in your life?

3. Where are your friends going at this point in their lives? Is that a direction you want your life to go? Do you need new friends? Are there friendships that you need to let go of (temporarily or permanently) because you are pulled into sin by these people?

4. Pray and ask God to help you start new friendships and take your current friendships that are just okay to a deeper level.

CHAPTER TWELVE

The Benefits of Blindness and other Practical Steps

> *27 "You have heard that it was said to those of old, 'You shall not commit adultery.' 28 But I say to you that whoever looks at a woman to lust for her has already committed adultery with her in his heart. 29 If your right eye causes you to sin, pluck it out and cast it from you; for it is more profitable for you that one of your members perish, than for your whole body to be cast into hell. 30 And if your right hand causes you to sin, cut it off and cast it from you; for it is more profitable for you that one of your members perish, than for your whole body to be cast into hell* (Matthew 5:27-30).

Above, we see Jesus use some pretty intense language about living a life of purity. He lets us know that it is not only wrong to have sex with a woman we aren't married to, but it is also wrong to desire and fantasize about things in our heart or imagination. He goes on to tell us that we should pluck out our eye or cut off our hand if it causes us to sin.

Jesus used extreme words here to cause us to think seriously about the effects of sexual sin. He isn't literally calling for people to chop off their body parts. But think about it. Would you do whatever it takes to get rid of sin in your life? If you really want to be free in your heart, won't you take the necessary steps to "cut off" sexual sin? Jesus teaches here that sexual sin is a heart issue more than a physical issue. If we take care of our heart, we won't need to sin with our bodies. But then He does something interesting. After addressing the heart issue, He gives us some practical advice on overcoming sexual sin. Most of this book is about dealing with the heart and mind. It is very spiritual and relational type of stuff. But in this chapter I want to share some practical things you can do to overcome sexual sin.

The way we can apply Jesus' words to our lives is to get rid of anything that causes us to sin. Here is a list of practical examples:

1. If you have any pornographic magazines, throw them away right away (don't give them away).

2. If there are catalogs or advertisements that are in your house for your sister, mom or spouse that cause you to sin, get rid of them and explain that you don't want this type of stuff coming in the mail or lying around the house because it is a source of temptation for you.

3. If you have a TV or a computer in your bedroom and you regularly watch programs that cause you to sin or look at websites that cause you to sin, move it into another room or just get rid of it. I even heard of a young man who was so fed up with giving into sexual sin that he chucked his computer out of his window, where it fell to its destruction. While I wouldn't recommend that you have to break your computer, I appreciate his passion to be free of sexual sin!

4. Keep a family computer in a shared living space where everyone can see what goes on with that computer. This helps keep everyone accountable.

5. Get accountability software on your computer, phone or tablet devices from x3watch.com by xxxchurch.com or Covenant Eyes at www.covenanteyes.com, where inappropriate websites are blocked or someone gets a list of websites that you visit.

6. If there are people with whom you engage in sinful sexual activity, cut off those relationships. End communication with them. Delete them from your phone, Facebook page, etc. Quit hanging out with them at school, work or parties. Explain that you are starting a new way to live your life and honor God and that you will not be able to spend time with them any longer. If you feel you need to apologize and ask forgiveness for your relationship, do it in writing or over the phone, if possible, and end contact after that. Don't keep entangling yourself with them!

7. If you go to a house where there is access to magazines or movies that cause you to sin, don't go there anymore. Don't go to sleepovers or to friends' houses during parties where people will pull out things that you know will cause you to sin.

8. Quit listening to music, reading books, and watching TV or movies that cause you to be depressed, discouraged or entice you to sin sexually. Throw those items away or delete them.

Hopefully you are getting the idea. There are practical things to do to keep you away from the source that can feed lust. As your heart is healed and restored in Jesus, the natural outflow is to part from these sinful practices.

Make a Covenant with Your Eyes

In Job 31:1, Job says, "I have a made a covenant with my eyes; why then should I look upon a young woman?" A covenant (in this case) is a solemn promise that you will not look to lust after women. It is an intense thing to make a promise that you won't lust after women with your eyes. But when you make a choice to honor God with the things that you look at, you will have His help to walk out this commitment.

I remember being frustrated sometimes and thinking, "Well, God, if you didn't want me to lust, why did you make so many beautiful women?" Sometimes it is easy to blame God or to blame women for dressing inappropriately, when it is really our issue. God invites us into a life of purity because with His help it is actually a possible reality. Remember, if you see a beautiful woman, it is not wrong to think she is beautiful or have a tempting thought about her. What is wrong is when you use your eyes to start studying her in a sexual way and think purposefully about sinning with her.

If you notice someone attractive around you and a sexual thought starts to arise, simply LOOK THE OTHER WAY and either get out of that place or start to focus on a Scripture that you have memorized. When your heart is committed to not look lustfully, you can start walking it out. One of my friends is pretty competitive, and treats this like a game. Every time he looks away from temptation, he regards it as a win! He doesn't like to lose, so this helps motivate him to honor God. A covenant with your eyes is not something to fear, but empowers you to make the right choice when temptation to lust comes your way.

USING THE "IT IS WRITTEN"

Jesus defeated Satan's temptations in the wilderness using the words of Scripture (Luke 4:1-13). After each temptation Satan threw His way, Jesus responded with, "It is written," and then quoted a Scripture verse. The word of God is powerful in defeating temptation! As I have encouraged you earlier in this book, write down Scriptures on a 3x5 card and quote that Scripture out loud when temptation comes. I remember being tempted to lust at work one summer with people all around, but under my breath, where no one but me, God and the devil could hear, I muttered a Bible verse I had memorized and got a smile on my face as that temptation was defeated.

USING PRAYER

Daily prayer is a powerful way to defeat temptation. I encourage everyone to cultivate the daily habit of spending time alone in prayer. I find that the morning is the most effective time for me. I don't always make time in the morning but that is when I prefer it. I can present my mind and my thoughts and my body to God. I can receive His love and hear His voice. I can ask God questions about my day at this time. I can also pray for the enemy's plans for me that day to be destroyed. This is a great time to read the Bible and spend time in God's presence as well.

On top of that, I think it is important to have a running conversation with God throughout the day. Friends have long times together or set appointments, but they also call each other, write letters, emails or send text messages back and forth during the day. That is what it should be like with God as well. Paul said in 1 Thessalonians 5:17, "Pray without ceasing." How can you pray without stopping? I believe by keeping your heart focused on God throughout your day and involving Him in everything. You can pray in the Spirit, ask Him questions about your coworkers, classmates, or experiences. You can just share what you are thinking. I encourage you to do this out loud whenever you can.

Praying throughout the day is also a powerful way to defeat temptation. When I really feel that Satan is coming after me in my thoughts, sometimes I start to pray over all my family or pray for all my friends and family that don't yet know Jesus. It's like I'm saying, "Fine, Satan, if that's what you throw at me, then I am going to throw this at you." And you know what? It works.

PHYSICAL AND CREATIVE OUTLETS

The Book of Proverbs is full of warnings about laziness. Being lazy can make it much more difficult for us to say no to temptation and flee from it. Set goals for your life, your week and your day. Make a schedule so you don't sit around aimlessly all the time. Plan some physical recreation like sports, bike riding, running or going on walks. Join a club or a team. Take some lessons in a subject that interests you. Develop hobbies like photography, writing, drawing, or collecting things. Spend your time in positive ways that give you physical and creative outlets.

The old school advice for overcoming sexual sin was to take a cold shower or going for a run when you felt sexually aroused (sometimes that was about all the advice was). While such advice alone is not enough to help you overcome sexual sin, there is still some truth to it. Change your body reactions by a cold plunge in the tub or the lake or go for a run. It's good to have a physical outlet for your body that is productive, healthy and fun.

If you fill your life with good, fun, creative and physical things to do, you will lessen your interest or available time in looking at pornography or trashy TV programs.

DEALING WITH LUST AND MASTURBATION

Some people believe that masturbation is a way to escape lustful passions. Actually, masturbation works against your purity. Masturbation has the power to imprint your lustful thoughts in your brain. David Kyle Foster, in his book *Sexual Healing*, stated:

> Those who engage in masturbation know very well it is a behavior that masters them. I've never had a person yet honestly claim to have control over his or her practice of masturbation. It controls them. It tells them who, when, where, what and how. It seduces them with immoral, erotic images of others—sometimes images so depraved that they can hardly believe their own minds.[22]

Some people think it is impossible for a man not to masturbate. Foster goes on to share, "There is no physical necessity in the human body to practice masturbation. Whatever a man's body needs to discharge, it does quite naturally with nocturnal emissions.[23] Sometimes guys complain about something that is referred to in slang as "blue balls," where their body is demanding sexual release and they can't seem to get rid of an erection. The truth, however, is that in the night your body will release semen if that is necessary. Of course, women deal with addictions to masturbation as well, though usually not for the same physical reasons as men. Like men, however, women too can become slaves to lust through masturbation.

There is much in the world that we live in to stimulate and tempt us sexually. Masturbation will only stir up more of a habit to think on things that are lustful. We are not supposed to feed lust through masturbation, but to RUN away from lust (2 Tim. 2:22). God will help you overcome an addiction to masturbation. Trust His grace to help you and make a commitment to break that addiction.

More information on this subject may be found in chapter 15, "FAQ."

ACTIONS STEPS

1. Goal planning. On a sheet of paper list a few goals to help stimulate your mind in such areas as Bible reading, Bible memorization, prayer, school, church, work, friendships, projects, fun, vacations, etc. Developing goals and working on achieving them gives you a positive way to spend your time.

2. Physical outlets. What are you doing to get physical exercise? Add some exercise, sports, walks or something else fun and recreational into your goals and schedule. Escape laziness!

3. Creative outlets. What do you enjoy doing that stimulates your mind? Spend some time singing, playing sports, playing games, hunting, fishing, painting, drawing, journaling, writing, dancing, collecting or creating.

4. Prayer for dealing with masturbation:

> Father God, I surrender my body to you as a living sacrifice. I confess my sin of lust and masturbation to you. I have given my body over to impure things. I ask that you would cleanse my body by the power of Jesus' blood. I present the members of my body to you as instruments of righteousness for holiness. Holy Spirit, help me with self-control. Deliver me from temptation. Let all that I think, say and do honor you, in Jesus' name, Amen.

CHAPTER THIRTEEN

Holy Fear

¹Therefore, having these promises, beloved, let us cleanse ourselves from all filthiness of the flesh and spirit, perfecting holiness in the fear of God (2 Corinthians 7:1).

¹⁴Pursue peace with all people, and holiness, without which no one will see the Lord (Hebrews 12:14).

If you love God, you should fear Him. The whole revelation of God's radical love and grace should not cause us to take lightly our relationship with God. In fact, the Bible says in Psalm 130:4, "But there is forgiveness with You, That You may be feared." The truth that God forgives us should empower us to fear God, not run off and commit more sin that we might be forgiven again.

There is a common misunderstanding about the grace of God that grace isn't grace unless it can be abused. The Bible, however, teaches that grace is given to the humble (1 Peter 5:5). In fact, grace actually teaches us: "For the grace of God that brings salvation has appeared to all men, teaching us that, denying ungodliness and worldly lusts, we should live soberly, righteously, and godly in the present age (Titus 2:11-12).

I want to emphasize that we need the radical mercy and grace of God. I would be nowhere without it. However, the power of God's radical love and acceptance in our lives should produce the fruit of holiness, a hatred for sin, and the fear of the Lord.

In her song, "Always on His Mind," Misty Edwards cries out to God, "How far will you let me go? How abandoned will you let me be?" This is a cry from a heart that has been radically touched by the wild grace of God. God's consuming love for us should elicit from us a response that doesn't ask, "How much can I get away with?" but "How far can I go with God? How abandoned can I become to this holy and awesome God?"

THE FEAR OF THE LORD

The fear of the Lord here does not mean having panic attacks about God. God doesn't want us to be afraid of Him in the sense of not approaching Him. God wants us to have an extreme respect and honor for who He is. Often people have a certain level of respect for their parents or their teachers (not everyone, but most people). Healthy fear means not doing anything deliberately to displease the one who is the object of that fear.

God sees, hears and knows everything. His eyes are always on us. This is not because He can't wait to punish us with the ugly stick every time we step out of line. It's because He loves us. He is involved. He wants relationship with us. Psalm 139 says that God knows when we sit down, when we rise up, and that He even knows our thoughts and the words we are going to speak before we speak them. My friend André taught me that one key to learning to fear the Lord is living with the concept that He is always watching. Live your life as before Him all the time, involving God in every moment, giving Him the place and honor that He deserves as a loving Father in your life.

There are so many promises in the Bible related to those who fear God. Here are some of them from the Psalms and Proverbs:

- "The fear of the Lord is clean, enduring forever" (Psalm 19:9a).

- "Behold, the eye of the Lord is on those who fear Him, on those

142

who hope in His mercy, To deliver their soul from death, and to keep them alive in famine" (Psalm 33:18-19).

- "The angel of the Lord encamps all around those who fear Him, and delivers them" (Psalm 34:7).

- "But the mercy of the Lord is from everlasting to everlasting On those who fear Him, And His righteousness to children›s children" (Psalm 103:17).

- "The fear of the Lord is the beginning of knowledge, But fools despise wisdom and instruction" (Proverbs 1:7).

- "The fear of the Lord is the beginning of wisdom" (Proverbs 9:10a).

- "The fear of the Lord prolongs days, But the years of the wicked will be shortened" (Proverbs 10:27).

- "In the fear of the Lord there is strong confidence, And His children will have a place of refuge" (Proverbs 14:26).

- "The fear of the Lord is a fountain of life, To turn one away from the snares of death" (Proverbs 14:27).

- "By the fear of the Lord one departs from evil" (Proverbs 16:6b).

HOW TO SEE GOD

Some Christians are under the impression that living in the fear of God and living in holiness are options for the really committed Christians or even for those that they deem a little "too intense" about their faith. However, the Bible is clear that holiness is not optional for the Christian. Hebrews 12:14 even goes to the extreme and says that without holiness no one can see the Lord. Could it really mean that? Could it really mean that you can't see God one day unless you live a holy life? I believe that it does.

The word holiness here has to do with idea of living a life that is set apart from the ways of the world and set apart unto God. We need to live a life of no compromise. God's word makes it very clear that taking the *eXXXit* from sexual sin is not optional:

> *¹Finally then, brethren, we urge and exhort in the Lord Jesus that you should abound more and more, just as you received from us how you ought to walk and to please God; ² for you know what commandments we gave you through the Lord Jesus.*
>
> *³ For this is the will of God, your sanctification: that you should abstain from sexual immorality; ⁴ that each of you should know how to possess his own vessel in sanctification and honor, ⁵ not in passion of lust, like the Gentiles who do not know God; ⁶ that no one should take advantage of and defraud his brother in this matter, because the Lord is the avenger of all such, as we also forewarned you and testified. ⁷ For God did not call us to uncleanness, but in holiness. ⁸ Therefore he who rejects this does not reject man, but God, who has also given us His Holy Spirit* (1 Thessalonians 4:1-8).

In this passage, Paul speaks very boldly about living a life that is set apart from the sexual immorality of the culture. He warns us that God avenges people who are defrauded by other people through sexual immorality. He goes on to say that if you reject this instruction for holiness, you are not rejecting man but rejecting God Himself.

It is important to note that there is only one way to live a holy life, and that is through what God has done for us through Christ by His grace. Holiness is a gift that we receive, and it is such a huge blessing to be invited into a life where we get to be like God in our character and conduct. Some people teach that we become holy by the good things that we do, but this is incorrect. Others teach that we can never really live a holy life and God just covers us for all the screw-ups we have along the way. This is incorrect as well. Holiness should not make us feel superior to other people; it is only by God's help that we can live holy. Holiness should not cause us to be stuck up but to serve others in love and compassion.

I love the Scripture that starts this chapter, 2 Corinthians 7:1: "Therefore, having these promises, beloved, let us cleanse ourselves from all filthiness of the flesh and spirit, perfecting holiness in the fear of God." This verse shows us that we are able to "cleanse ourselves from all filthiness of the flesh and spirit, perfecting holiness in the fear of God" but it is only by the "promises" that we have received from God.

Shortly before Paul's strong warning in 1 Thessalonians 4:1-8, that we read above, he wrote:, "And may the Lord make you increase and abound in love to one another and to all, just as we do to you, so that He may establish your hearts blameless in holiness before our God and Father at the coming of our Lord Jesus Christ with all His saints" (1 Thessalonians 3:12-13). Paul is affirming that the Lord causes us to increase in love for others and that He is the One that establishes our hearts in a holy life. Holiness doesn't come from trying to live a better life in our own strength. It comes as a response to the love of God and the work of the Holy Spirit. As we know what Jesus has done for us and grow in His love, we use the help of the Holy Spirit to "put to death the deeds of the body" (Romans 8:13). As you grow in the "width and length and depth and height- to know the love of Christ that passes knowledge" (Ephesians 3:18-19) you can be "filled with all the fullness of God" (Ephesians 3:19). When you truly get to know God and how much He loves you, you become complete on the inside and start to set apart your life, literally separating yourself from things that displease God because you are in a love relationship and want to bring extreme honor to the one you love.

The late pastor and author John Wimber used to teach that it is helpful to view "holiness" as "wholeness." Indeed, wholeness is a very helpful aspect of living a holy life. This is the idea that is presented when the Bible calls us to be "perfect." The word "perfect" often means "complete" in the Bible. We will live a holy life as we become complete in Christ Jesus.

So holiness really comes from the love and grace of God at work in our hearts, where we become complete and respond by separating ourselves from sin in our attitudes and actions. We are not called to separate ourselves from people of the world or go live in a cave somewhere. We are supposed to live in the midst of the world and yet shine as a light that points people to Jesus.

> *12Therefore, my beloved, as you have always obeyed, not as in my presence only, but now much more in my absence, work out your own salvation with fear and trembling; 13for it is God who works in you both to will and to do for His good pleasure.*
>
> *14Do all things without complaining and disputing, 15that you may become blameless and harmless, children of God without fault in the midst of a crooked and perverse generation, among whom you shine as lights in the world, 16holding fast the word of life, so that I may rejoice in the day of Christ that I have not run in vain or labored in vain* (Philippians 2:12-16).

The apostle Paul saw salvation and purity as gifts from God, which He works in us, but also that it is necessary for us to work out what God is working in us. We do not become holy by our works, yet our obedience to God is of the utmost importance. Obedience is our response to God's grace. Sin still matters to God after we come to Christ. We see God's warnings to the 7 churches in Revelation chapters 2 and 3. Some of these churches had given in to sexual immorality and He warns them that they will face extreme discipline if they do not repent from their ways. First John 5:21 warns us to keep ourselves from idols. If we are not repenting of sin and we let idols into our lives as believers, we are fooling ourselves if we think that this doesn't affect us or our relationship with God. We need to turn from these things by God's grace, repent and allow God to transform our hearts.

Holiness is an invitation into a life full of joy and freedom. You are invited to hate the things that God hates and love the things that God loves. It is not bondage to live the way that God calls us to live. Holiness is not for the goody-goodies; it is a provision that God has purchased through the blood of His Son Jesus. No matter how unholy you may have lived, you can turn over a new chapter in your life because of the blood of Jesus. By the power of the cross in your life, you can live a life that honors God.

> [13] *Therefore gird up the loins of your mind, be sober, and rest* your *hope fully upon the grace that is to be brought to you at the revelation of Jesus Christ;* [14] *as obedient children, not conforming yourselves to the former lusts,* as *in your ignorance;* [15] *but as He who called you* is *holy, you also be holy in all* your *conduct,* [16] *because it is written,* "Be holy, for I am holy" (1 Peter 1:13-16).

THE PURPOSE OF HOLINESS

God hasn't called us to live a life of holiness in the fear of the Lord because He wants to kill our fun. He hasn't done this to give us some impossible standard by which we will always fail. As John shows us:

> [1]*Behold what manner of love the Father has bestowed on us, that we should be called children of God! Therefore the world does not know us, because it did not know Him.* [2]*Beloved, now we are children of God; and it has not yet been revealed what we shall be, but we know that when He is revealed, we shall be like Him, for we shall see Him as He is.* [3]*And everyone who has this hope in Him purifies himself, just as He is pure* (1 John 3:1-3).

The reason to live pure and holy before God is because we are going to see Jesus one day, and we are called be like Him. Every

147

Christian's calling is to become Christ-like. We are "predestined to be conformed to the image of His Son" (Romans 8:29). Our highest honor in life is to become more like Jesus. Jesus has purchased us and forgiven us by His grace, but growing to be exactly like Jesus in every way is a lifelong endeavor.

GLORY

Our highest motivation for making the *eXXXit* out of pornography and sin is for the glory of God. The Westminster Catechism says that "Man's chief end is to glorify God, and to enjoy him forever." The highest purpose we have in life is to yield ourselves to our Maker and say back to Him, "You know what I was made for, and I give my trust, my heart and all of my life to surrender to your glory." In *The Weight of Glory*, C. S. Lewis said, "To please God… to be a real ingredient in the divine happiness… to be loved by God, not merely pitied, but delighted in as an artist delights in his work or a father in a son—it seems impossible, a weight or burden of glory which our thoughts can hardly sustain. But so it is."[24]

I challenge you to look at the commandments and instructions in the Bible as invitations to living for the glory of God and coming alive to your true purpose. The law can be a heavy thing for us to try and live up to if we live in our flesh. But if our hearts are full of God's love and we are convinced that He really has our best in mind, we can learn to take delight in the ways that He calls us to live. We are then able to say along with the Bible, "His commandments are not burdensome" (1 John 5:3b).

God invites us to "present [our] members as instruments of righteousness to God" (Romans 6:13) and "present [our] bodies a living sacrifice, holy, acceptable to God" (Romans 12:1). "Therefore, since we are receiving a kingdom which cannot be shaken, let us have grace, by which we may serve God acceptably with reverence and godly fear. For our God is a consuming fire" (Hebrews 12:28-29).

Just think about it. No matter where you have come from or what you have done, God has grace to cleanse you and give you a new heart. You can live a righteous and holy life now and give God glory with all that you are and all that you do. This is the great adventure that you were born for: GIVING GOD GLORY AND ENJOYING HIM FOREVER! May a passion for a life of purity, a life that is Christ-like, burn in you like a fire!

PRAYER

Father God, thank you for your plan and provision for me to live a holy life. Thank you that it is only through what you have done by your grace that I can live a holy life. I renounce all self-efforts of striving for holiness in my flesh. I thank you that holiness is a gift and I present my body to you as being alive from the dead and as an instrument of righteousness to you. In every thought and motive I pray that you would be delighted. I yield my mind to you. I want to see You and all things that are pure and good. I set my mind on things above. I present myself to you as a living sacrifice, holy and acceptable. Burn in me, O Consuming Fire. Thank you for a love that burns like a fire. Thank you for a passion to live for the greatness of Jesus' name. God, you are transcendent and holy, yet you are so near to me. Let everything I do and say bring you glory. I love you, God. In Jesus' name, Amen.

CHAPTER FOURTEEN

End Human Sex Trafficking —Get Porn-Free

[18] The Spirit of the Lord is upon Me, Because He has anointed Me To preach the gospel to the poor; He has sent Me to heal the brokenhearted, To proclaim liberty to the captives And recovery of sight to the blind, To set at liberty those who are oppressed; [19] To proclaim the acceptable year of the Lord (Luke 4:18-19).

Near the start of Jesus' ministry, He enters a synagogue in Nazareth and it just so happens to be the day that a pre-determined Bible reading is going to be recited from Isaiah 61. Jesus is handed the Book of Isaiah to read this passage, which is quoted above from Luke chapter 4. After reading the passage, Jesus informs the people that He is the fulfillment of this ancient prophecy. He is the One who would "heal the brokenhearted… proclaim liberty to the captives…and set at liberty those who are oppressed."

Central to the message of Jesus in the Gospels, and even to many passages in the Old Testament prophets, is this theme of justice for the oppressed. From my research on pornography I have learned that women in the pornography industry are really oppressed, much like slaves. They are not just beautiful, wealthy women who enjoy having sex for a living. Often, they have been abused and forced to do many things against their will. You may not be aware of this, but prostitution is being run worldwide as well, which keeps women bound like slaves. This insidious and horrible trade is known as human sex trafficking. These are exactly the type of people Jesus came to set free and give an *eXXXit* out of their bondage. Jesus wants spiritual slaves set free, but He also came to set literal slaves free!

WHY TALK ABOUT HUMAN SEX TRAFFICKING IN A BOOK ABOUT PORNOGRAPHY?

I wanted this in my book because I believe God has led me to include it. For one thing, there is a very strong link between the two that I believe has greatly not been explored. Boys, even before middle school, are being exposed to pornography at alarming rates. I have learned from someone inside the U.S. Dept. of Labor that as early as high school (potentially even middle school) young men are being recruited to lure girls in their school who fit a certain profile (no dad, sexually active, certain risk factors) into prostitution and sex slavery. Our young people need to be made aware of what is going on in their world. This is an alarming issue that many of us may prefer to ignore. However, ignoring it will not make it go away. Each of us and our children need to be made aware of this and related issues so that we can make a difference.

THE TRUTH BEHIND HUMAN SEX TRAFFICKING.

Although general awareness of the problem is growing, you may not know that worldwide slavery is still a huge problem. It did not end with Abraham Lincoln and the Civil War. There are more slaves in the world today than at any other time in history. Millions of people all around the planet are forced to be slaves for labor and/ or sex. Human sex trafficking involves individuals who are forced to work as a slave in some form of sexual exploitation. Judging by the research I have done, human sex trafficking and prostitution are virtually inseparable. The documentary *Nefarious: Merchant of Souls* presents a clear and compelling case about the problem.[25]

Below are some statistics on human sex trafficking taken from the *Nefarious* documentary website:

- Governments estimate there are 27 million slaves being held worldwide—more than at any point in human history.(U.S. State Department, March 2012)

- Sexual exploitation makes up 79% of identified forms of human trafficking, including prostitution, forced stripping, massage services, and pornography. (United Nations Office on Drugs and Crime, Global Initiative to Fight Human Trafficking, 2009)

- 88% of these victims are women and children. (UN Office on Drugs and Crime, 2009)

- After drug trafficking, trafficking in humans ties with the illegal arms industry as the second largest criminal industry in the world today. It is the fastest growing. (U.S. Department of Health and Human Services, 2011)

- Most sex trafficking is regional or national and is perpetrated by traffickers who are the same nationality as their victims. (United Nations, Global Report on Trafficking in Persons, 2009)

- As many as 2 million children are subjected to prostitution in the global commercial sex trade. (U.S. State Department, Trafficking in Persons Report, 2011)

- At least 15,000 people are trafficking into the United States annually. (U.S. State Department, Trafficking in Persons Report, 2010)

- Approximately 600,000 to 800,000 victims annually are trafficked across international borders worldwide. (U.S. State Department, Trafficking in Persons Report, 2011)

- Estimates suggest as many as 300,000 children annually are at risk of commercial sexual exploitation. (Richard Estes and Neil Weiner for University of Pennsylvania, 2001)

- The average age of entry into prostitution in the United States is 13- to 14-years-old. (Sara Ann Friedman for ECPAT-USA, "Who Is There to Help Us?," 2005)

- Nationwide there are fewer than thirty safe homes for victims of sex trafficking to receive treatment and services. This severe shortage regularly causes their inappropriate placement in juvenile detention facilities. (Streetlight Tucson, 2012)[26]

How Human Sex Trafficking and Pornography are Related

Human sex trafficking and pornography are heavily related. I want to share a few reasons with you as to why this is. First of all, both involve organized crime. In many nations organized crime rings work to abduct, break down, and sell women into sexual slavery (as seen on *Nefarious: Merchant of Souls*). An Attorney General's Study on Pornography found that 85 percent of pornography is controlled by organized crime.[27]

Secondly, sex trafficking and pornography are related in that people who use pornography may become unsatisfied with just watching pornography and start to look for prostitutes to satisfy their lusts. A study conducted by a group in London found the following about men who were involved in using prostitutes:

Fifty-eight percent of these London men used pornographic film and/or videos at least once a month. Fifty-one percent used Internet pornography once a month or more often (20% once a week; 15% more than once a week). Thirty-two percent of these London interviewees used pornography in magazine form once a month or more often. While using pornography, 60% of these men reported that to some extent they classified the women in pornography as a prostitute. Monto and McRee (2005) compared the pornography use of 1,672 U.S. men who had been arrested for soliciting women in prostitution with samples of U.S. men who had not used women in prostitution. Men who had used women in prostitution were far more likely to use pornography on a regular basis. In a statistically significant linear relationship, men who were repeat users of women in prostitution were more likely than first-time users of prostituted women to use pornography, and first-time users of women in prostitution were more likely than non-buyers to have used pornography.[28]

Lastly, the common ground that sex slavery and pornography share is that they both share the same spiritual root, the sin of lust. Both of these sins bring forth the same result: death (Romans 6:23). After watching *Nefarious: Merchant of Souls* I was deeply disturbed because I realized that there is one thing that would wipe out sex slavery overnight. And that one thing would be men denying their lusts and refusing to demand sex when, how and where they want it. It would end if men treated women like the apostle Paul said to Timothy, to treat "older women as mothers, younger women as sisters, with all purity" (1 Timothy 5:2). Sex slavery and pornography exist because men desire to use women for their own selfish and sinful lusts. Yes, women are involved in lust as well, but the majority of what drives this whole thing is the sin that rules men's hearts.

HELP END SEX SLAVERY, GET PORN-FREE

So what can you do to make a difference against human sex trafficking? Well, you can do a lot of things. You can raise awareness by sharing resources, stories and films. You can organize prayer meetings and ministries to intercede on behalf of this great epidemic. You can and should give to organizations that are on the frontlines helping rescue victims and bring justice through law. You could even join the military to be trained in combat and later join law enforcement agencies that combat human trafficking by rescuing girls and arresting pimps and traffickers. But the number one thing you can do is deal with the lust in your own heart and make the *eXXXit* from pornography to purity!

It is inconsistent to wage war against human trafficking while continuing to live in a pornography addiction. You shouldn't stop waging war against trafficking, but you need to wage war against sexual sin in your own life. It's time to show men that to get to the heart of this issue is to deal with things on an individual level. It may not seem very practical, but at the heart of all the pain that this epidemic is causing is unchecked sinful desires. We can make a difference in this fight by surrendering the slavery of our own hearts to Jesus. If you get set free by Jesus from pornography, you are making a difference in helping to set a sex slave free.

OUR ONLY HOPE

Our only hope to see a difference in human trafficking and pornography is the hope that comes through Jesus Christ. Sin leaves us hopeless. As I referenced above, "for the wages of sin is death"; however, the rest of the verse says, "but the gift of God is eternal life in Christ Jesus our Lord" (Romans 6:23). The power of what Jesus offers us is a new heart and a new identity.

How then are we to make a difference in the world around us? Surrender to Jesus and He will give you new desires. (Please review this in chapters 3-6). Next, we as the church can pray and be a voice of love and mercy to those who have used pornography, been involved in the sex industry, purchased prostitutes or been a prostitute. When we realize that we all need Jesus and He really is the hope of every heart, we can extend forgiveness to those who seem untouchable. Remember, Jesus Himself said, "Those who are well have no need of a physician, but those who are sick. I have not come to call the righteous, but sinners, to repentance" (Luke 5:31-32).

To close this chapter, I want to share with you a beautiful story about how sharing the love and kindness of Jesus with someone in the sex industry can make a difference and offer real hope.

SARAH'S STORY

Several years ago I helped start an outreach team at my church, Sonrise Christian Center, called the G.O. Team. The G.O. Team goes out into the community to visit houses, stores, coffee shops, the homeless and the addicted. We love on people, pray for healing, hand out socks and hygiene kits, bless homes and ultimately share the hope we have in Jesus Christ.

One particular night as we were heading out, one of the ladies on the team, Sarah, told me that she really had on her heart a desire to visit some of the "bikini barista" stands in our community. Not far from our church are several of these coffee stands where women wear bikinis, lingerie or less as they sell coffee in these little drive-thru huts. At least some of these "bikini barista" stands have been known to be fronts for prostitution. So, Sarah took a couple of other women with her to share the love of Jesus with girls serving coffee in bikinis.

Sarah arrived at the first stand and got out of her car. She was quickly greeted by a man asking her what she was doing there (she didn't pull up to the window like you usually would in a drive-thru stand). He was the owner. The other women in the vehicle were caught off guard but stayed inside the car and prayed. Sarah said, "I'm here to visit the girl working in your stand." He replied, "Well here, come on in then," as he opened up the door to the coffee stand.

Sarah walked in and the door closed behind her. The barista was a thin young woman, probably in her late teens or early twenties, wearing only a bikini and covering herself up in shame. Sarah quickly shared with her, "I'm Sarah, and I'm from a church in the area. I just came here to bless you. Is there anything that I can pray for you about?"

The girl was a little bit surprised and thought for a second. "There is something; it's my mom. She is battling cancer. You can pray for my mom. And by the way this job is temporary, I just really need the money." Sarah knew she was embarrassed and didn't seem to enjoy working there.

Sarah prayed a prayer of blessing over this young barista and prayed in faith for her mother to be healed in Jesus' name. The barista began to cry and reached out and gave Sarah a big hug. Sarah asked her, "Have you ever gone to church or known the Lord?"

She replied, "Yes, when I was a young girl I used to go to church. I used to believe."

Sarah told her, "If you believe in Jesus, then you are God's child and God has plans that are good for you, plans to give you a future and a hope (Jeremiah 29:11). God has something better for you than this. God loves you so much." She then pulled out a pink Bible she bought that day and said, "I have a special gift for you."

The barista looked amazed and just reached out and grabbed the Bible like a little kid getting a birthday present she had really been longing for. "For me? This is for me?" She reached out and gave Sarah another big hug. Here was this loving Christian woman, embracing a young bikini barista and sharing with her the power of God's love.

Sarah blessed her on her way out the door. As she left, the owner walked up to Sarah and mumbled, "I take good care of these girls." A spirit of boldness came over Sarah and she said firmly, "You call this taking good care of these girls? Let me ask you this: do you have any daughters? Would you let your own daughters work out here? You put these girls in all sorts of danger!"

He replied, "Well, at least I don't make these girls have sex with me before they work here like those other barista stands."

Sarah said, "Well, that's good that you don't make them do that. But this is still wrong. Do you believe in God? Do you believe in Jesus? I want you to go home and pray to God and ask Him what he thinks about what you are doing to these girls!"

After this rather intense exchange, Sarah got back in the car with the other women and drove off. They continued to pray for this young barista who had encountered the love of Jesus. Sarah drove by several times over the next several weeks to follow up with this barista, but never saw her car or her there again. We believe that was the moment she ended up making the *eXXXit*.

It is through sharing the love and truth of Jesus with hurting people, both the producers and consumers in the sex industry, that many of them discover an *eXXXit* from sex slavery and into freedom!

CHAPTER FIFTEEN

FAQ

Wouldn't pornography help me learn about sex so I am better for my spouse?

Believing that pornography will help you become better at sex with your spouse is like thinking that stealing money will train you how to become a better banker later in life. Learning how to use sex wrongly through pornography will not help you use it well. You need to understand that pornography has an addictive element to it that changes the way you think. The Bible likens sin in Romans 6:23 to a slave master that pays out death to its slaves. Pornography will not help you be better at sex; it will enslave you and cause death in your marriage later on.

It is amazing to me how many married couples who are having sexual problems have turned to pornography for "help." You need to remember that pornography uses actors who pretend and often are forced to make things appear as though this is the greatest way that sex occurs. As you read through chapter 2, "Sin with a Capital 'S,'" you can see how destructive pornography is to people. If you think you can use porn and stop the day you are married, you are deceiving yourself; it is *highly* unlikely you will do so. For instance, pornography conveys the idea that women will always enjoy whatever a man wants to do sexually, whenever he wants it. But women have a monthly cycle, and if you don't treat a woman well and know how to approach her in the proper way, sex can be painful for her. What's more, if you use pornography, you will bond sexually to pornography rather than bonding to your spouse. Many women report having a problem feeling sexually satisfied in a relationship because their husbands are consulting pornography rather than the Bible or sound books written by Christian psychologists or physicians.

I urge you, do not think of pornography as a helpful teacher, but as an armed criminal trying to rob you of your future marriage relationship.

My dad is the one who is giving me pornography. What should I do?

This is a very difficult situation to be in, I'm sure, and I am very sorry that you have found yourself in this situation. It sounds like you desire to be free of pornography. First of all, I would pray for your dad and forgive him. Make sure that you approach him in an honoring way, even if he is the one that is directly or indirectly supplying you with pornography.

After making sure that your heart is right towards your dad and being able to honor him, have a talk with him and let him know that you don't like the effect pornography is having on you. Tell him what God is doing in your heart and the reading you have been doing that has been shaping your decisions. Don't approach your dad in anger. Make sure, to the best of your ability, that you continually refuse to be in a place where you will have access to his pornography. The Bible says "the wrath of man does not produce the righteousness of God" (James 1:20). In other words, being angry with your dad won't help him live a righteous life. You need to honor your parents (Ephesians 6:1-3) even if they are doing something sinful with their lives. You are not honoring them for their sin, but honoring them as your parents, and in doing so you honor God and bring blessing on your own life.

Lastly, you can even encourage your dad to get some help or to read this book. It will take courage for you to have a talk like this. I commend you for wanting to do the right thing. It isn't right that a child should have to approach his parents about something like this, but even then, God can bring something good out of this. Remember, you aren't responsible for the choices your parents make. You are responsible to love them and honor them.

There is no one as a young man (or woman) that I can talk to about this problem. What do I do?

I remember feeling the same way when I was going through my teen years. If a parent, pastor or mentor in your life has never talked with you about pornography or related issues, you may get the impression that it is too embarrassing to talk about with anyone. I encourage you to start praying about who you can talk with concerning this matter. God will provide someone for you. You can talk to a godly parent or a pastor. If that isn't a possibility, tell your parents that you want to have an appointment with a Christian counselor or doctor. They talk to people about these things all the time and won't think you are weird for having questions.

Ultimately, you are probably facing a fear about opening up about such a personal area in your life. Most parents or pastors would help if you said, "No one has ever talked with me about sex and I need some help. I have some questions." God doesn't want you to figure out this stuff on your own but to have His help and the help of others. Remember, "God has not given us a spirit of fear, but of power and love and a sound mind" (2 Timothy 1:7). Reach out until God provides you with a relationship where you can find answers to your questions. If possible, I encourage you to try your parents first. I encourage you to read this book as well and keep reading your Bible. The Bible has a lot to say that will help you understand how to handle sex and relationships.

Isn't using pornography a normal part of my sexual development?

It is normal to have a sex drive, but using pornography will not help you develop sexually. The human race survived thousands of years without pornography. One of the largest misconceptions about pornography is that it is a helpful guide or a helpful teacher. Research and science prove that pornography damages its users. The Bible tells us that sin pays the wages of death (Romans 6:23).

You should not feel ashamed or dirty for desiring to have sex or that you have thoughts about sex. However, if you look to fulfill those desires and thoughts outside of God's righteous standards in marriage, you will negatively affect your sexual development. God created our sex drive and He knows best how you should use it. Don't let the culture hijack your view of what will help you sexually.

I'm a pastor (or youth pastor). Do you think it is really my job to talk with young people about sex?

I do not believe that as a pastor or youth pastor that you are to be the primary voice that instructs young people. Youth and children should primarily be instructed by their parents. But I do believe that you are to be one of the most important voices to young people on this issue after their parents. The reason you should be one of the top voices is because God is very clear on this topic. From Genesis to Revelation, God speaks very clearly on the topics of relationships, marriage, sex and sexual sin.

My dad used to tell me, "When the Bible speaks loudly, speak loudly; when it speaks softly, speak softly; and when it doesn't speak, don't speak." By applying this advice, we will have to speak loudly. First of all, I recommend encouraging parents to be the primary voice that speaks to their children on sexuality. Second, as you preach and teach from the Bible, apply what it says to the modern issues we face about sexuality. Times change, but the root issues of sexual sin are still the same and are still solved through the Word of God.

Lastly, if you won't speak clearly with conviction about God's standard for sex, who will be the voice of truth in our culture? Too often, parents don't speak up, and between the media and the sex industry, children and youth are getting misguided information.

What age is the right age to have "the talk" with my child?

I suppose the answer to this question depends somewhat on your child. But I firmly believe that parents, to the best of their ability, should be the first to speak to their children about sex. You need to have a bond with your child that allows you to have openhearted conversations with him or her about sex and any other topic of a sensitive nature. I am concerned that sometimes young people would not have stumbled into pornography if they had had a concerned parent there to answer questions. Sometimes curiosity leads children to explore things, but you don't want your child exploring the internet or a friend's brain for answers on sex.

When we look at the Book of Proverbs, we see a dad who really wanted his son to know about the dangers of sexual immorality and temptation. Proverbs 22:6 reminds us that if we train our children in the way they should go, they won't depart from it when they are older. This certainly applies to training them in the area of sex as well. Train them; take the initiative and don't just wait for them to come ask you things. They may never come on their own.

Sometimes there is a concern that if you bring up the subject of sex, you will make them more curious. Do you remember what things were like for you when you hit puberty? Everyone is born with a sex drive. Sometimes we have to face up to reality and realize that our children are going to have questions about sex because they are wired to.

I recommend talking with your children before they hit puberty and before they find out about sex from their peers (which will happen even if you send your kids to private school or if you home-school). The latest I would start the ball rolling here is around age 10. Sometimes an earlier age may even be necessary or wise. There are resources available that start sharing age appropriate sex information for children as young as the toddler years.

Lastly, people used to refer to the "birds and the bees" talk. Our thinking about this really needs to change. We need to move from having a "sex talk" to having a running conversation from childhood into adulthood. With all the media and all the buzz words floating around young people, there is a need to talk several times (maybe even several times a month) with your child about sexual things. The old way was a one-time talk, but the new and necessary thing to do is to have an open door policy with your child that goes through the years. Make sure not to act embarrassed or to shame your child for having questions. It is great that they trust you enough to bring you questions. Make sure to pursue them as well and have a heart connection with them, so that they know they can trust you with such a sensitive topic as sex.

Additionally, you may want to take your child out to dinner or on a special night away to make this a memorable part of his or her emergence into adulthood.

I have a 13 (or 15 or 18) year old son, and I think he already knows about sex. Do I still need to talk to him anyway?

Yes, absolutely, you should talk to your child about sex. You may approach the topic a little differently with a statement like, "I want to have a talk with you. It probably should have happened a few years ago, but I would like to talk with you about sex. You may know some of the things that I am going to say, but there is a lot more to learn than you might think."

Even though I was using pornography and thought I had heard everything there was to know, I still had a lot of questions as I approached marriage. I still counsel men who are about to get married or are already married who still have questions about sex. It is never too late to talk with your child about sexual things.

If your child knows about sex already and it wasn't from you, there is a really good chance that they received bad information that likely will motivate them to handle sex outside of God's ways. They need to have their mind renewed as Romans 12:1-2 instructs us. You can help renew their perspective by talking openly with them.

I hear people at school talk about sexual things but I don't know what they mean. I can't talk to my parents about it, so who should I talk to?

I would challenge you to honor your parents (Ephesians 6:1-3) and go to them first. Your parents probably don't realize that you even have questions like this. Give it a try and say something like, "Dad (or Mom), I need to ask you a question and it feels a little embarrassing. Guys at school are saying _____. I don't understand what they mean. Can you tell me please?" Tell them that you need to be able to have open conversations with them and that you want to ask them so you get the truth, rather than getting information from your friends or on the internet. If that doesn't work out, I would encourage you to find a pastor, mentor, doctor or a counselor you can go to.

Is it okay to masturbate?

This is a very common question. Almost every guy I have talked with has struggled with this issue and it is more and more common for women to struggle with it as well. Although masturbation is common, it is not a good idea. First of all, masturbation almost always is accompanied by lust and sexual fantasy. In 1 Corinthians 6 we read that those who are sexually immoral won't inherit God's kingdom.

Since masturbation reinforces sexually immoral thoughts and behavior, it is sinful.

Masturbation causes your brain to bond very strongly to whatever you are thinking about at that time. This causes sexual problems in people's brains. Sometimes people think they will just masturbate until they get married, but this can become extremely addictive. You don't set the boundaries on addiction. I have heard many times of married couples having struggles because masturbation did not stop with marriage.

Masturbation is really self-sex that teaches you to fulfill your own sexual desires in your own ways on your own time. For men, this is problematic in marriage. Typically, a woman needs more time and relational intimacy to achieve sexual climax, but men can achieve it very quickly. Masturbation trains a man's body to have an even quicker sexual climax, which can negatively affect the wife.

Some married people believe that it is okay to masturbate once they are married as long as they focus on their spouse. I would caution married couples not to participate in sexual activity that does not actively involve both of them.

My husband is looking at pornography; what can I do to help him?

I am so sorry to hear that this is happening. It is great that you want to help him. For starters, I want you to know that this is not your fault. It is not right for any man to use pornography, but it can be especially damaging in a marriage because you may feel like you aren't doing something right to please your husband. Men who are addicted to pornography usually aren't involved in it because they are displeased with their wives. This is not to make an excuse for them. But you need to know that it isn't your job to get them out of this. You can help them, but it is not your fault or your ultimate responsibility.

First, you should pray fervently for your husband. Second, make sure anything you do towards your husband is in an attitude of honor and respect. Ephesians 5:33 says "let the wife see that she respects her husband." It may seem very difficult to respect your husband if he is living in sin. You do not respect him for what he does; you respect him in order to honor God. At times, direct confrontation will be necessary, but be respectful of him as a man and as your husband. If you nag him and talk in anger to him, you will only push him away from you and, probably, deeper into pornography. Men are wired to respond to respect.

Thirdly, don't withhold sex from him. Sex should not be used as a weapon in a marriage. Paul warns in 1 Corinthians 7 that if sex is not regular, then Satan has an opportunity to tempt the couple. This doesn't mean that it is the woman's fault if sex doesn't occur every day or that a husband should demand sex based on this passage. Paul is encouraging regular sex as a deterrent to temptation.

Fourthly, confront your husband in an attitude of respect and share with him your deep hurt over this and how you want to help him. Let him know that you are willing to stand by him and walk through this if he is willing to get help. Encourage him to read this book and talk with a pastor or counselor.

If your husband is unwilling to get help, if you see no change, or if he is abusing you in any way, get help from a pastor or counselor for yourself. You need to take care of your own heart through this process even if he is or is not willing to get the help he needs.

I am married and my wife and I were thinking that watching pornography together would enhance our lovemaking. Is this a good idea?

This is not a good idea at all. Even if you have good motives because you think this will help you, there are many negative consequences that can arise from this. There is a very good chance that one or both of you will open yourselves up to lusting over the actors in the pornographic films. With pornography you will be inviting a perverse spirit into your bedroom. Remember that the people in pornography are actors who are being paid to make things appear a certain way.

I believe that Hebrews 13:4 often is misinterpreted when it says, "Marriage is honorable among all, and the bed undefiled; but fornicators and adulterers God will judge." The "bed undefiled" means that sex between a husband and wife is a good thing, but it doesn't mean "anything goes." When you rent or purchase or click links for pornography you are helping finance fornicators and adulterers, which is clearly condemned in the verse above. You are also financing the rape, abuse and mistreatment of women, not to mention the human sex trafficking industry.

If you truly feel that pornography helps your sex life, then in the nicest possible way I want you to know that you have a problem—a sin problem—and you need help rewiring your heart and mind according to the word of God. I don't mean to shame anyone who has done this, but you need to repent and pray and build intimacy as a husband and wife God's way.

I am in a position of influence and am totally bound to pornography. What should I do? If I admit to what I am doing, many people will be hurt.

The most important thing you can do in a position of influence is deal with the sin in your life and get healthy in your relationship with God. Honoring God is more important than any position you can have before men. There are many avenues these days for getting help and reaching out to people who will be truthful and compassionate. There is no way to really deal with this problem alone.

The Bible is clear in Proverbs 28:13, "He who covers his sins will not prosper, But whoever confesses and forsakes them will have mercy." Find another pastor, leader or counselor who will work with you in a redemptive way. It may seem painful to open up and tell the truth, but it is the first step to freedom. God is so amazing. He can bring redemption in the midst of our darkest situations.

As a leader you have a responsibility to God and the people under your influence to deal with issues in your life. It's not too late for God to heal you and restore you. Don't believe the lie that if you conceal this, things will be better for people. Depending on what is really going on in your life, you may not need to make a public statement. A situation like this is really case-by-case and needs wise and godly people involved. May God grant you the courage to humble yourself and reach out for help.

What do you mean by "eXXXit?" Is it really possible to get over a pornography addiction?

What I mean by "*eXXXit*" is that you can be free from the dominating desire that drives you regularly to look at pornography. I do not mean that you can get to a place where you are never tempted or that you no longer have a sex drive. But you can stop looking at pornography and you can come to a place of wholeness and holiness where you no longer give in to temptation. These are the promises of God that give us this truth, as we have looked at in this book in Romans 6, 1 Corinthians 6, Ephesians 4 and Colossians 3.

God really does provide all the tools we need to make the *eXXXit* out of porn. If you believe and embrace the gospel and how it changes your heart, let God heal you and obey God's instructions to reach out to others for confession and prayer. You *can* walk in freedom from pornography. It's not about focusing on being porn-proof as much as it is focusing on becoming like Jesus.

I feel like all I think about is sex. How can I change my thoughts?

Well, you may have a strong sex drive and if so, you will certainly need to learn to manage those desires. As I shared earlier in this book, a teacher I had used to always say, "What you starve, dies, and what you feed, grows." In Colossians 3 Paul told the church there to set their mind on heavenly things. He went on to tell them to put away sinful things from their past lives and put on new things that come from God, such as love. You need to be aware of the influences in your life and cut off things that influence you to think about sex more often. I assume you are single when asking this question. As you cut off negative influences, start spending time with God in prayer and in His word, and spend time doing healthy things for fun and building good friendships. Also, when you pray, commit your thoughts to God every day. He will help you.

It is important not to give up and to commit to a spirit of no compromise. Be vigilant in this area. Don't tolerate temptation. Don't allow thoughts to linger that should not be in your mind.

I don't see what the big deal is about a little pornography and masturbation while I am single. I'll be married eventually and I won't need this stuff anymore, right?

Well, that might be your intention, but you are deceived if you think marriage will take away your sin. If you use "a little pornography and masturbation" you need to realize it might turn into using it a lot. You aren't training yourself for your spouse; you are training yourself to respond to pornography and masturbation.

Being free from sexual sin is a result of what Jesus has done and a work of the Holy Spirit (1 Corinthians 6:11). Respond to God's grace while you are single and live a life of purity. That is the best gift you can give your spouse. Don't look for marriage to bail you out of sin and addiction. Look to God and to His ways.

I don't feel that alarmed as a parent that my son uses pornography. I mean, it kind of makes me feel good to know that he likes women and that he has a healthy sex drive. Aren't you being too hard on young men? Boys will be boys, right?

I hope that I have been clear that it is normal for people, especially young men, to have thoughts about sex. But it is not "healthy" for anyone to use pornography. Sometimes parents get excited that their child experiments sexually and they are relieved that the child "functions" sexually. Don't be deceived, though. When anyone fulfills their sexual desire outside of marriage, they open themselves up to many negative consequences, such as a lack of intimacy with God, addictive behavior, STDs and an inability to bond in healthy relationships.

We need to raise up boys who go against the grain of the culture. Don't settle and believe that "boys will be boys." Instruct young men in the right way by giving them purpose, vision and a cause worth fighting for. I love how in the Book of Daniel we see 4 young men who go against the culture they are in and honor God. God promotes them for being young men who stand out from the lifestyle of everyone else. Encourage your son to stand out and not just fit in to what "everyone else is doing."

I homeschool my children and they are pretty sheltered. I don't think they need to know about this kind of thing until they are out of high school. What are your thoughts on this?

I applaud homeschoolers'; it's hard work! As of the writing of this book my wife and I are homeschooling our oldest of 4 children and about to start the next one. I believe that all of my advice applies equally to homeschoolers as it does to any other family. If your child goes to church, watches TV, plays sports or goes anywhere in public (department store, grocery store checkout stands or mini-marts) they are going to see, hear and read about sexual things from an early age. The admonishments in Proverbs to raise our children in sexual purity apply to all families. And while there may be a few environments that are more controlled, such as homeschooling, temptations and improper information can still reach a child no matter their school model. Be proactive instead of reactive.

Endnotes

1. Mark and Grace Driscoll, *Real Marriage: The Truth about Sex, Friendship and Life Together* (Nashville: Thomas Nelson, 2012), 110-120.

2. This truth is unfolded in greater depth in Kris Vallotton, *Moral Revolution: The Naked Truth about Sexual Purity* (Shippensburg: Destiny Image Inc., 2011).

3. Pornography Statistics taken from http://www.internetsafety101. org/Pornographystatistics.htm

4. Ron Luce, *Battle Cry for a Generation: The Fight to Save America's Youth* (Colorado Springs: David C. Cook, 2005), 77, quoting from "Pornography Targets the Teenage Brain, Mind, Memory and Behavior: America's Children versus the Impotence Industry," a report prepared by Judith A. Reisman, Ph.D., the Institute for Media Education.

5. *Ibid.*

6. Dr. Philip G. Zimbardo and Nikita Duncan, "'The Demise of Guys': How video games and porn are ruining a generation" http://www.cnn.com/2012/05/23/health/living-well/demise-of-guys/index.html

7. Ted Roberts, interview on ICSEX, http://vimeo.com/16984617.

8. William M. Struthers, *Wired for Intimacy: How Pornography Hijacks the Male Brain* (Downers Grove: InterVarsity Press, 2009), 64-65.

9. *Ibid.*, 85

10. Naomi Wolf, "The Porn Myth," *New York Magazine*, October 20, 2003, http://nymag.com/nymetro/news/trends/n_9437/

11. Pamela Paul, *Pornified: How Pornography is Damaging Our Lives, Our Relationships, and Our Families* (New York: Times Books, Henry Holt and Company, 2005), 90-91.

12. *Ibid.*, 80.

13. Ron Luce, *Battle Cry for a Generation*, 85, quoting from "The Science behind Pornography Addiction," a speech delivered by Dr. Judith Reisman at a science, technology, and space hearing on November 18, 2004. Her entire speech is available at http://commerce.senate.gov/hearings/testimony/.cfm?id=1343&wit_id=3910

14. Daniel Weiss, "Pornography, Infidelity and Divorce," http://www.citizenlink.com/2012/02/21/pornography-infidelity-and-divorce/

15. David Kyle Foster, *Sexual Healing: A Biblical Guide to Finding Freedom from Sexual Sin and Brokenness* (Ventura: Regal Books, 2005), 206.

16. http://www.europrofem.org/contri/2_04_en/en-viol/81en_vio.htm. from http://en.wikipedia.org/wiki/Physical_abuse.

17. Justin and Lindsey A. Holcomb, *Rid of My Disgrace: Hope and Healing for Victims of Sexual Assault* (Wheaton: Crossway, 2011), 28.

18. *Ibid.*, 31.

19. Ted Roberts, interview on ICSEX, http://vimeo.com/16984617.

20. http://www.forbes.com/sites/danschawbel/2012/02/14/10-memorable-quotes-from-the-start-up-of-you/

21. Ted Roberts, interview on ICSEX, http://vimeo.com/16984617.

22. David Kyle Foster, *Sexual Healing*, 220.

23. *Ibid.,* 221.

24. C. S. Lewis, *The Weight of Glory and Other Essays* (New York: Macmillan, 1980), 13.

25. Website http://nefariousdocumentary.com/learn-more/

26. From Nefarious: Merchant of Souls. Website http://nefarious-documentary.com/learn-more/

27. David Kyle Foster, *Sexual Healing*, 205, citing Michael J. Mc-Manus, ed., *Final Report of the Attorney General's Commission on Pornography* (Nashville, TN: Rutledge Hill Press, 1986).

28. http://embracedignity.org/uploads/Men_Who_Buy_Sex_and_What_They_Know.pdf

Online Resources Page

Porn Scar
A ministry to help people get free, stay free, and free others
pornscar.com

XXX Church
Blogs, accountability software, tools, and outreaches
xxxchurch.com

Mastering Life Ministries
Articles, testimonies, resources, books from David Kyle Foster and more on freedom from multiple sexual issues
http://www.masteringlife.org

Moral Revolution
A ministry of Bethel Church, articles, Q and A, books, events and much more
www.moralrevolution.com

Covenant Eyes
Articles, resources, and accountability software
www.covenanteyes.com

Enough is Enough
Protecting children online, resources, statistics and more
enough.org

Porn Harms
Morality In Media is the leading national organization opposing pornography and indecency through public education and the application of the law. This site includes current information on cultural and legal issues relating to pornography and sex crimes.
www.pornharms.com

Exodus Cry International
Creators of the award-winning Nefarious *documentary on Human Sex-Trafficking. A prayer and advocacy movement to end human trafficking.*
http://exoduscry.com

Not for Sale
Their mission is to create a world where no one is for sale.
http://www.notforsalecampaign.org

International Justice Mission
Legal and advocacy work to stop and prevent human trafficking
http://www.ijm.org

Freedom in Christ Ministries
Books and resources on Breaking Free from Strongholds and Establishing a Deeper Identity in Christ
http://www.freedominchrist.com

Lifestyle Christianity
Teaching from Todd White on Identity in Christ
www.lifestylechristianity.com

Neck Ministries
Teaching from Dan Mohler on Identity in Christ
www.neckministries.com

isonrise.org
John Hammer's home church, Live Stream, preaching audio, conferences and resources

Ministry Information

To stay in touch with John Hammer's ministry and creative projects, or to invite John to come speak and minister for your event, please check out the following resources.

John's home church and audio of John's sermons, available for free:
www.isonrise.org

Blog, Itinerary, Updates, Speaking Requests, etc.:
www.thefreedomletters.com

YouTube Channel for videos of John's spoken-word poetry:
www.youtube.com/johnandhammer

Facebook:
www.facebook.com/johnandhammer

Twitter:
www.twitter.com/johnandhammer

Instagram:
instragram.com/johnandhammer

eGenCo

Generation Culture Transformation
Specializing in publishing for generation culture change

Visit us Online at:
www.egen.co

Write to: eGenCo
824 Tallow Hill Road
Chambersburg, PA 17202 USA
Phone: 717-461-3436
Email: info@egen.co

facebook.com/egenbooks

youtube.com/egenpub

egen.co/blog